GROWING NORTH

At 27 Miles per Hour

A Memoir by
JOHN BRUHN and JIM JULISON

To our wives: Deb and Deb

Preface

Memory is an interesting thing. It bends and adjusts as the keepers grow and change. When two friends get together to reminisce, memories develop into great stories and adventures. Especially if the donuts are good and the coffee pot bottomless.

We, Jim and John, love sharing our adventures with readers in the way we remember them, which, incidentally, is not always quite the same with each telling, or even with each teller. Our memories are as unique as our very DNA, but, perhaps, a bit more prone to mutation. As with all storytelling, the adventures grow and take on a new meaning as each telling breathes new life into old memories. So, beware, when we walk our pet alligator down the sidewalk on a cold fall day, realize it could have been a hot summer afternoon or a breezy spring morning. Who knows for sure which way it happened? The important thing to know is that somewhere there was, indeed, an alligator being walked by someone and that someone is probably one of us, and most likely, someone in the story learned some sort of something along the way.

You might say it began as the high school class of '75 graduation day came closer for us and we contemplated what came next. It was over the winter break of '74 that we started to talk about what we wanted to do before we moved on to what we knew would be real adulthood. Something we would always remember and perhaps something that would set the stage for and how we wanted to live the rest of our inevitable settled lives.

We got anxious as the big day of graduation arrived. Our jitters had nothing to do with the pomp and circumstance of the ceremony. We busied ourselves with plans to embark on the adventure. We planned our trip beyond "Where no man has gone;" further than the wilds of the Yukon. A friendship that began before we had words to express friendship could surely weather a trip beyond the great beyond.

As soon as we tossed our graduation caps in the air and returned our wrinkled gowns, we headed north.

Contents

In the Beginning

It started when the two lifelong friends John, and Jim decided to spend some time in the wilderness backpacking "Where no man has gone before" (as the saying goes) in the wilds of the Yukon. Now the Yukon itself was not remote enough for these two and they had decided it had to be North to the Arctic Circle because, after all, anybody could go to just the Yukon. Jim had spent many summers on the beach in the upper peninsula (UP) of Michigan and dreamed of unexplored coastal areas. So, Jim harbored a secret goal of walking on the beach of the Beaufort Sea to explore the coast and the flotsam that must be there that has never been seen by the common beach-combers.

We were born in 1957 at the tail end of the Baby Boomers generation. And grew up in a new subdivision no more than thirty miles from the City of Big Shoulders or the Windy City as the politicians called it, in what is now considered a Northwest suburb of Chicago.

Their subdivision, "Dunhurst East" or, as they called it just "Dunhurst" was located at the intersection of Dundee and Elmhurst roads in the village of Wheeling. Back then it seemed to be the norm by which subdivisions and shopping malls were named. We were practically on farmland. They spent many a summer day playing in the then-vacant fields surrounding the subdivision. The houses were built before nearby shopping was available. Nowadays it's not a problem to load up the car and drive to wherever you wanted to go. But remember, this was not at a time when every home had two cars. That was a very rare sight to see. So, for almost everyone, the shopping was done on the weekend or after dinner.

Eventually, developers built a small strip store with a "National" food store, a "Ben Franklin" and a drug store. We each lived in a small 900 square foot, three-bedroom, one-bath Cookie-cutter homes, nearly as unimaginative as the brand-new subdivision. The only distinction between the homes was the color choices each homeowner picked out. As time passed landscaping grew and garages were built by our fathers and the neighbors, and everything started to look different.

We were part of the suburbia migration. The GI Bill loan program guarantees made loans for these less expensive homes possible, but you had to be prepared to move out to areas surrounded by farm fields and without the hustle and bustle of the big city, but that might have been the draw everyone was looking for. Our parents were looking for the image that was portrayed in Life Magazine: the perfect house with the picket fence and kids playing in the yard. The kind of home that Ozzie and Harriet lived in with their two perfect teens, Dave and Ricky.

Our Korean War veteran fathers were about the same age and had married about the same time and, of course, had kids about the same age. Almost all the fathers were hard-working Blue Collar, nine-to-five men who worked hard during the day but were eager to get home to their family and friends. Maybe because of their military training they were able to work as a team and get the job done. How did they do this in civilian life? They talked to their neighbors and found out who worked in the same area and started one of the first carpools.

As John was told each person in the four-person carpool would put enough gas in his car to get to work for one day. This would cover four days and the fifth day would be whatever pocket change they could scrape together. Their wives would also benefit and be able to use the car if needed for three or four days. It was a win-win for everyone.

The fathers worked Monday through Friday, leaving Friday and Saturday nights open to, let's say to let their hair down. This was a car-pool party for the upcoming week but was also open to all the neighbors. John's house had a one-and-a-half-car garage, with the half turned into a screened-in porch. There was a long table in the center that could seat ten to twelve people. Everyone who came over brought a dish to pass and there was no judging if someone could not bring anything. It was so different than living in the city. It was like an old-world smorgasbord with neighbors substituting for family.

With the creation of the "subdivision" came new opportunities and challenges. The days of multiple generations living together in one house became a thing of the past. This was a time of independence, or so they thought. Now everyone had to rely on neighbors they did not previously know. Neighbors became a family by proximity. When you saw someone working outside, you offered to help. If someone's kid did something wrong the neighbors would be there too, let's say correct the problem. Sooner or later, you were going to need the favor returned.

Neighbors got to know everyone's strengths and weaknesses. They pooled their efforts and started to make their new prefab house into a home. As kids, we had chores to do and if we did not do them, there was hell to pay. But when they were done, we could go to our "set limits" and explore and make friends. There were only two rules that could not be broken. Be on time for meals and be back home when the streetlight came on.

When we say "set limits," we mean how far we could travel away from our front porch.

When we were very young it was a line of sight up and down the street, no turning corners. After that, it was the block, around all four corners and back yards. But it was a long time before we could cross the highway to another subdivision. So, we almost exclusively stayed to ourselves until junior high. We were surprised to find out later in life that the kids in the surrounding subdivisions were afraid to enter "Dunhurst" as it was considered a rough neighborhood.

Every kid from kindergarten through sixth grade walked to the Mark Twain Elementary school, right in the center of the development. Excellent suburban planning meant no busses were needed to get all the students to class; everyone could easily walk. Walking to school meant no one had to walk more than a mile or two. Yes, indeed we walked to school, all by ourselves. We were big boys, already six years old. Although still not old enough to participate in Wheeling's annual rattlesnake hunt. It didn't matter if the weather was rain, snow, sleet, or one hundred degrees, we walked. If the postman could do it, so could we. At least it wasn't uphill both ways like our parents had to deal with, along with the six or ten miles to walk, depending on who told the story to whom.

We first met in the first grade. We were seven, walking to school. John lived a block (not a real city block, but a burb-block) farther away from the school than Jim. At the first road crossing, we met up with another friend, Brian who lived at that corner and the three of us walked together to school. A year or so later we added the fourth Rob, who lived just around the corner from John. They met while playing in their backyards through the white picket fence that divided the two properties. After a sense of balance developed, they could join all the other kids that would walk on the top 2x4 board holding the fence

4

together. It might not sound like a lot of fun, but fences were like a secret path through all of the backyards. When you have a bunch of kids all walking the fence, in different directions, you now have a game called "king of the road" or "medieval jousting."

The school years were pretty much the same blurry routine every day for the first few years. Only the books changed from *Dick and Jane* to *Tom Sawyer* and the arithmetic tables changed from addition and subtraction to multiplication and division.

In First Grade, we turned seven, lost most of our front teeth, and got introduced to Cub Scouts. Cub Scouts changed everything outside of school. Oh, the activities. All the new Cub Scouts enjoyed doing the same type of new activities. The moms made the dads get involved as leaders, which, despite some grumbling, turned out pretty good because the dads bonded as much as the kids did. Maybe they had an immediate bond because of all they went through in the war, that they could never talk about. Or maybe it was the bonds of fatherhood that made even them believe in that old TV show title, "Father Knows Best." We didn't care; all we boys saw was that everyone had a great time.

Well, as we aged, Cub Scouts led to Webelos (We Be Loyal Scouts) and that brought us into Boy Scouts. By the time we turned eleven, got an oversized set of permanent teeth, and entered Sixth Grade, the world of Boy Scouting opened the door to overnight camping trips, field trips, and everything outdoors.

When it came time to advance to a full-fledged Boy Scout, we had to go to a new meeting location with new leaders and kids from other subdivisions. Our dads also followed us. In our minds, they were progressing just like we were. Right along with us, our dads began their ascent to leadership roles in Troop 212.

At the first meeting, we were assigned to the "Wolf Patrol." The guys were ok, but they were together for a few years and had lost a few members of their patrol to age, or as the leaders used to say "They were lost to one of the two liquids – Perfume or Gasoline." Around junior high, most of the guys lost interest in the Boy Scouts. The only ones who stayed in around high school were the ones who were going for their Eagle Scout rank. Only four percent of Boy Scouts achieve this honor. The "Wolf Patrol" had established a pecking order that was going to be hard to get into. So, we just kind of followed what they were doing and learned how a patrol worked; like how many boys do you need to form a patrol? What is every patrol required to do and what positions needed to be filled? Right along with us, our dads began their ascent to leadership roles.

As we learned the ropes, and more kids from Dunhurst joined our patrol, we decided to split off and form our patrol. The "Alligators" were born. An alligator was our mascot and yes, at that time you could buy an alligator. We bet you didn't see that coming.

We named him Charlie. He was about a foot and a half long with very sharp teeth. Each scout in the troop knew Charlie's teeth were sharp because each of us learned the hard way. We all got bit feeding Charlie. We finally wised up and used new-found skills learned in our leather-making activity to make a leather alligator handling glove, which we wore to feed Charlie. Later on, we leveraged our skills to earn a merit badge for leather-working.

As the" Alligators" developed our dads immersed themselves fully in our troop. Their leadership brought a new breath of life to a downward spiraling troop that was not that old. Looking back at some of their "new life" ideas, one particular activity says it all: The Galena Jamboree

We had many outings but only one camping trip each month. The last one of each year was called a Jamboree. We never actually looked up the definition until all these years later: a large celebration or party, typically a lavish and boisterous one. Boy Scout Jamborees could be local, state-wide, or national.

Jamborees tested the skills of the Boy Scouts, but more importantly to the leaders, Jamborees provided a chance to show off. When we turned twelve. We'd be in Junior High in the fall. We had almost outgrown Boy Scouts. When the scoutmaster got the itinerary, all the assistant scoutmasters became dead set on making it one that would be talked about for years to come.

Galena hosted a parade down Main Street and invited all the troops to represent. The scoutmasters got together and came up with the greatest plan we ever heard of. We were going to have them participate, not as a bunch of kids trying to walk together in step. We were going as a drum and bugle marching band; did we know how to do this? No. We had no idea. The scoutmasters probably thought that if the army could turn a bunch of knuckleheads into a well-trained unit in eight weeks, they could do the same with a bunch of pre-pubescent boys in the same amount of time.

The first step was to get a commitment from the troop who agreed to attend the Jamboree. Everyone jumped right on board with what the dads presented as the greatest show on earth. Next, we had to learn how to march in step.

If you think this is easy, think again. Straight walk, turns, starting, and stopping all take time to learn. That, semi-mastered, the scoutmasters determined who was going bugle and who would drum. No one knew how to play except for one kid that was a drummer in the last couple of years of grade school. Where did he come from? Neither of us remembered him as part of Troop 212. We think one of the other dads brought in a "ringer".

Eugene, a well know classmate of ours had a dad that was not one of the leaders. Eugene's dad was in the army marching band and knew what was needed and what we could get away with. He came up with something akin to a magic show. Your brain knows it can't be true but your eyes keep telling you something different. The boys holding bugles were part of the show, but not part of the music.

Music training was for the other two kids who were going to be drummers along with the "ringer." They practiced on the tabletops until they were playing as one. It was a good thing because those two brought their drumsticks home and practiced for hours on end. Two boys practiced "playing" the cymbals with garbage can lids. At one point one of the parents wanted to pull their kid out because of all the non-stop noise. The leaders had no idea how to handle this new aggressive behavior to achieve perfection.

So, troop 212's Drum and Bugle Corps consisted of; two boys walking with a banner stretched out between them in front of the whole group advertising to everyone just what they were about to see. About three steps back there were three flag bearers, one holding the national ensign in the center, and the state flag and the Boy Scout flag on the outsides. Next, two steps back were the, pardon the term, musicians. Two boys on the outside of the second row with real cymbals to replace their garbage can practice cymbals and the three drummers between them with the ringer in the center. The third row had five buglers that were for show only but looked like they were ready to start playing at any time. The rest of the troop fell in behind the buglers one step back and filled in four or five rows. And just like that Troop 212 became a drum and bugle corps.

After weeks and weeks of marching, it was now only two weeks away from the Jamboree. The leaders pulled in all their resources and called the entire troop in for a pre-trip meeting, in uniform, for inspection. Everyone met outside the building in the parking lot for a big surprise. There, laid out on tables, were items that were procured from the high school and Great Lakes Navy Base. All the instruments and flag poles were on loan for the big event. Little did we know that our parents secretly bought all the kids red baseball jackets, all from the same store so they could negotiate a great deal. Even if some of the kids could not afford one, everyone chipped in a little and had a jacket. The troop leaders and Eugene's dad said they needed something more to make it all pop. So, the troop bought white web belts and white spats for everyone to wear. We guessed they were planning on doing a lot of marching going forward!

The flag bearers were also given the white pole holders that they wore around their necks that would hold the flagpole in a pocket for long marches. We spent the next few hours getting fitted and the whole group headed off to a full-dress rehearsal.

All the moms and dads that could make it were there, taking pictures as everyone marched like little toy shoulders up and down the high school parking lot, making turn after turn, stopping and starting like we were doing it for years. The scoutmaster was leading with all the assistant scoutmasters flanking the outsides. They not only did this for the looks but just in case someone passed out from overheating. You see, it was still summertime and hot. It was going to be a long day and a longer parade route than we have ever marched before. On the day of the parade, we all took our positions. Everyone was in their olive drab green boy scout uniform with long pants, with a red baseball jacket and a white web belt and spats. The "music" was just a simple marching cadence by the drummers with a bang from the cymbals every so often.

As we marched past the reviewing stand, the flaggers dipped their outside flags while the national ensign remained upright and the rest of the troop with an "eyes right" command, turned their heads toward the mayor as the crowd cheered. Everyone up and down the street joined in for the yelling and cheering for the little group from Wheeling. Troop 212 received numerous awards that day and we became the talk of the campground.

That night just before dusk, someone came running up to the leaders asking for one of our buglers to play tap's while the national ensign was being lowered. We'll never know how they weaseled out of that one.

The following month there was a parade in our hometown that we participated in every year. This time we were going as the new marching band. Due to the extreme heat, the red jackets were not worn and a bunch of the kids did not attend. Needless to say, it did not pack the same punch as the Jamboree.

We don't know for sure, but most likely our common interest in the outdoors formed during our early years camping with our families, plus our scouting experience. Forty-five years later, we still go on an annual canoe trip for a weekend, where we practice a few of the skills and lessons learned but mostly we just enjoy the company of old friends and stay well-oiled with alcohol and tell the stories of our many adventures.

The Adventure Begins

As High School graduation day came closer, we became more and more anxious. Not about the graduation, but due to the impending adventure we were about to embark on.

We spent many hours at our high school hangout, the Golden Bear restaurant, five miles away in Buffalo Grove, a nearby town, where we would drink endless cups of bitter coffee that set us back twenty cents a cup. Buffalo Grove had also built a new high school and our school, Wheeling High School's students were split our sophomore year because it was well past maximum occupancy, giving the students in the area the option to go to the new school or finish at the high school they started in. For some reason, most of the girls went to the new school and we didn't so, we spent most of our free time at or around the new school, where the ratio was a cool 5 girls for every boy. The Golden Bear was within 200 yards of the school, so it was easy for the girls to sneak away, and not too far for us to cut out and drive to. We knew all the waitresses, partly because we were there all the time and partly because the girls that used to go to our school, worked at the Golden Bear part-time.

Besides being where the girls were, we planned and revised our plan, until the Golden Bear imposed a one-dollar minimum, and we had to move to Denny's in Palatine another mile up the road. We knew most of the waitresses for all of the same reasons.

Eight weeks earlier we enrolled in a night course on wilderness survival with the world-renowned survival instructor Ben Crabtree. Ben is one of the largest people you may ever meet. He is just under seven feet tall and weighs in at 315 pounds without an ounce of fat. When he talks his voice is so deep, without trying. He is the type of person that commands the attention of everyone around him for 100 feet. We kind of pictured him as the typical meat-eating mountain man that would eat cooked or raw meat as he pleased. Due to his size and crude grizzly bear-like mannerisms we called him our carnivorous instructor but the group just called him "Big Ben" or Ben to his face. He accepted both and was still working on picking his teaching moniker for this type of audience. When backpacking it is called a "trail name" and it can only be given to you, you cannot pick your own. We think anyone who knew him was afraid to give him a trial name just in case he didn't like it.

Ben held the class at night for four weeks at Dryden elementary school in nearby Arlington Heights. Dryden was part of the school building boom to accommodate the baby boomers at that time, it was expected a new school would be named after a famous literary figure in history. John Dryden was a poet from the 1800s best known for his satire. An ironic twist for us, but of course, when we got there, Dryden was just the name of some guy in the ancient past.

As we entered the classroom, memories of 1st grade at Mark Twain Gramer School flooded our brains. The intoxicating smell of mimeograph paper almost put us in a trance for the entire day. When the teacher handed out the freshly prepared assignments we looked around and we weren't the only ones under the influence of the ink. Mark Twain also brings back some not-so-good memories.

One of the kids in our class, Eugene, was a little quiet and not laughing like normal for him for almost a week. Then one day he just stood up and walked to the back of the classroom and without altering his step, pulled out a large paperclip, unfolded it into u shape, and jammed both ends into the ungrounded electrical outlet. The lights flickered for a moment until they went off completely. The smell of burning flesh sent the girls in the back row into vomiting spasms. The next few moments created a chain reaction that would send any janitor into a nightmare that they would talk about for years to come.

As all the kids were slowly being led out of the classroom you could see the nurse and office staff rushing into the room. The janitor was doing his best with the small brown papered package of magic sawdust that they used to sprinkle over such a mess. It would help for one or two kids but there were many in the chain reaction from almost all the girls in the back half of the classroom.

As everyone was running around trying to do something, Eugene just stood there holding his hand with no expression on his face. It could have been "shock" or maybe there was something deeper. Maybe he did not get the results he was hoping for. This was beyond the nurse's basic job duties and needed more attention than she could offer with her limited supplies of band-aids and aspirin. The principal grabbed Eugene, put him in his car, and drove him to the nearest doctor who was about forty-five minutes away.

There were no local emergency services for something as minor as first-degree burns to a finger and thumb. In hindsight, maybe the principal thought taking Eugene to the doctor was better than dealing with the mess back in the classroom.

Eugene didn't come back to school for two or three weeks. Our teacher thought moving Eugene's desk to the front of the class would prevent a reoccurrence, his new seat was set far away from all outlets. He never talked about what he did but, everyone wanted to see his scars and he would slowly open his hand to all the attention a war veteran might receive. We are not sure if it was a good or bad thing but, the attention was short-lived and over the next few weeks and months just about everyone forgot what happened. Sure, everyone remembered the event but, when the kids talked, they just said "you remember what that kid did" or it was about all the chaos surrounding the event. It could also be he just wanted some attention, and this was the best he could think of. Unfortunately, his injures were diluted by all the playground injures, after all a broken arm or leg was a lot more interesting and surprisingly more common considering how crude the playground was.

We had a diverse group in our Wilderness Survival class: several people were older, about to retire and prepare for life in a motor home; others were going to apply the knowledge gained to family camping excursions; while a few, like us, we're planning high adventure.

We had the same desks for our Wilderness Survival class as we did back when we were students at Mark Twain Elementary School: steel-framed with a wood top and seat all in one immovable piece. Not much room for a grade-school kid, let alone a grown teenager and overweight adult. If "Big" Ben would have tried to sit in one of them, he might have decided to make other arrangements for us.

As soon as we squeezed into our seats, Ben began his lecture.

"It is important to ensure you have plenty of twine in your survival kit at all times."

An attentive student in the first row asked, "How much is enough?"

"5,000 feet," Ben, with a commanding voice, replied without batting an eye.

A startled voice from the other side of the room remarked "This compact survival kit will end up being the size of "Cleveland!!"

Ben shot a stern look at the startled student and said," I suppose 500 feet would be enough for a very basic kit." His gaze seemed a little less stern. Perhaps he realized his mistake. We left the class that first night with images of a large 90-pound spool of rope in a survival kit in our heads.

Ben was a famous wilderness survival instructor. He also trained the Apollo astronauts in survival for NASA. We wondered what possible skills could you learn about outdoor survival on earth that would help you in space? We can remember him recounting stories about spending six months in the Sahara Desert, and six months in the Amazon Rain Forest. Ben described with an enthusiastic twinkle in his eye how he would spend his entire six-week vacation every year alone in the Okefenokee Swamp with nothing but a knife and his survival kit. A precursor to the TV show, "Naked and Afraid."

Ben could not have known the ramifications of teaching us about snare traps. He explained that in the next class we would all be demonstrating some of the traps we were instructed on.

One of the students, Brian arrived before we did at the next class. As we took our seats Brian enthusiastically prepared for Ben to arrive; eager to demonstrate what he had learned. Brian set snares all over the room. A very startled Ben got caught in one of Brian's snares as he came in the door, and turned toward the teacher's desk, as he tried to untangle that one, his face became serious and he bounced into another one attached to the desk chair. His expression changed from serious to angry just before he was caught in another attached to the chalkboard, and then another on the pencil sharpener, after rebounding in and out of several traps he began to snarl. He ripped the last one apart taking the pencil sharpener right off the wall.

Ben took a few minutes to regain his composure and speak. The clear "Try-line" high test fishing line used for the snare traps did an excellent job, as Ben was a rather large quarry. Ben did not ask who set the traps but after he had time to consider the workmanship, he congratulated the class on the handy work and suggest that future snares should lift the target off the ground to prevent the escape like the one he had made.

We learned various fire-building techniques and were told to return the following week with a bow, stick, and kindling when we were instructed to use this equipment to start a fire. We looked at each other, the sprinklers on the ceiling, and at thirty-five students working feverishly to start fires in an elementary school. Luckily nobody produced much more than hot sticks, so remained dry, protected from the school's fire suppression system. To this day, we wonder if Ben knew the futility of the exercise and what he was teaching us the value of dry matches.

At the end of the formal training sessions, Ben organized a campout at a local forest preserve, just outside of Rockford, so that we would all have the opportunity to test and hone the new skills that we had acquired.

We loaded Jim's Jeep with all the necessary gear. We tried to keep the gear to the minimum to show Ben that he trained us well. We also made sure we brought our newly acquired equipment to have the opportunity to break it in, as well as our survival kits.

We had never been to this particular campground before so, we were full of anticipation as we drove the Jeep through the park entrance. We couldn't help but be stricken by the number of people and groups in the place.

We entered the park and slowly snaked our way down the road behind a long caravan of campers of every description. We noticed the number of motorcycles was inordinately high. We passed large groups of individuals that looked as though they were preparing for a long night of drunken debauchery. Everyone's site had a campfire burning and smoke hung heavy in the air, mixed with an occasional breeze carrying the smell of the pines. This had the same effect of a sickening sweet-smelling Glade air freshener over cigar smoke.

As we came to the final turn before the end of the road, we saw Ben wearing gigantic plaid shorts and sandals, dragging a couple of picnic tables (one in each hand) over to his trailer. The brakes on the Jeep squeaked to a stop next to Ben, pulling his attention away from his task, looking over at us. A smile came to his face as he recognized us.

"Have any trouble find'n us?" he asked.

Without waiting for an answer, he pointed to a field beyond the road we just drove in on where half a dozen tents were already set up.

"You guys can set up anywhere over there," he said.

We found a suitable spot in the open field he pointed to, some distance from the rest, as more students were expected to arrive. We wanted a little space out of sight so we camped in the most secluded area we could find. We wanted the cover of trees, but there were no wooded spots available in our group area.

Over the next couple of hours, the rest of the students trickled in and set up their tents and equipment. We sat in the grass in front of our tent watching the spectacle of the strangest collection of would-be campers we had ever seen.

The Greco brothers came in with their CJ5, with a roar coming from giant chrome glass pack straight thru mufflers, playing Heavy Metal music that was almost as loud. Then in came the guy we called "Hat Guy" because we never knew his name, but he always had a hat on. After he set up his tent, he drove stakes around his tent at about ten-foot intervals creating an area, not unlike that of a surveyed piece of ground. He strung a rope from one stake to another, creating a sort of border around his campsite. Next came the meticulous Sherman Wilson. We were completely astounded when from out of his 1971 Ford Maverick trunk, as if not to be outdone by Hat Guy, came small, 18-inch-high sections of white picket fence which he set up around the real-estate that he claimed for his campsite. The only person who was missing was Brian. Maybe Ben did not invite him because of the classroom snare trap incident?

As the day went on Ben called everyone together for a simulated survival exercise. Each team was given a packet that contained instructions, with compass headings and distances to be paced off. We were told to follow these directions and find what was at the end, the first team to find their destination was the winner. The competitiveness of the group began to show, everyone, chomping at the bit to get started.

Ben said "Go!!" and everyone opened their packet, got out their compasses, and started every which way, even though the directions in each packet were identical. That caused us to pause. Did we each get different directions? Or were they the same? After some head-scratching, because the directions seemed clear as day to the two of us, we took off North.

After several hours of treasure hunting, the entire group gave up and began straggling into the campsite empty-handed. We blamed the obvious, wrong instructions.

As the sun began to set in the west, the motorcycle group in the next campsite began getting louder and more raucous. We decided to go to our tent site and cook up some canned stew and relax. We had a nice little fire and were satisfied with our dinner and began to roll a "J" when out of nowhere a guy claiming to be a ranger popped out from behind the Greco's Jeep. He demanded the bag that had been quickly crotched. We gave it up as we could do nothing else, but were quite embarrassed and worried about how this would turn out. Would we be going to jail? Would Ben's outing be ruined?

It turned out that this ranger was somehow connected with the motorcycle group and rejoined them to enjoy our stash leaving us with a final threat to keep our mouths shut. Leaving us hang-dogged and angry with nowhere to put it.

It was a very turbulent night as we tried to sleep, the group, or what was now turning into a motorcycle gang, got loader and drunker. They began drag-racing on the road we had come in on starting in front of our group's campsite.

Ben's trailer was closest to their site. So, he was receiving the brunt of all the commotion that was bordering on mob action. Maybe it was his military training or just the way he was brought up. At any rate, Ben decided that he was the one that could fix the situation. Most of our group peeked out of our tents waiting to see what Ben was going to do.

Ben walked over to the group like he owned the park. He had an air of authority about him and his size didn't hurt. He was in charge and not to questions. This was something that we had not noticed about him in the classroom setting. We also never did know what his rank was in the military but, it was rising in our imagination as we saw him in action.

Ben walked right past the outside ring of loudmouth twenty-year old's and past some very large, quiet guys that just watched him. He marched right up to someone that he picked out to be the leader. By the way, it was not the guy we mistook for a park ranger. We could not hear what Ben said but we sure could hear the "yes sir" coming from the guy he was talking to. It was like he was talking to his drill sergeant in basic training. Maybe there was a military bonding, or maybe, just maybe Ben was his drill Sargent, who knows? Maybe they were just mocking him.

The whole group did start to quiet down, a little. As Ben walked past the park ranger want to be, who by the way was so stoned he could not stand up, Ben just shook his head in disgust. He went back to his trailer and we all tried to get some sleep, even though there was very little improvement in the situation.

In the morning we found that Ben's campsite had been vandalized and his boom box was found in a nearby creek. So, his authority only lasted as long as his presence.

We began to pack up to leave after a short breakfast of ham and eggs over the fire, thanking Ben for the experience and saying goodbye to the classmates that lingered. Some had hightailed it out of there, quietly leaving at the crack of dawn, before the sun began to bake the grassy area that we were camped on. We finished loading and fired up the Jeep. Feeling a little sad, we slowly return to the road and continued out of the park knowing we would probably not see any of them again, all that faded away as we began to talk about our future adventure. This was a practice run, a small precursor to what lay ahead.

Planning the Route

We knew where we wanted to end up and approximately what time we wanted to arrive. But we had so much to see along the way. After all, there was an Interstate Highway system that was started about the same time we were born, by President Eisenhower, and pretty much completed by the time, we were ready to leave. It seemed almost prophetic. But who would know all the new roads and what were the amenities along the way?

The Chicago Motor Club A.A.A! They have been around helping travelers since 1906! If anyone would know about cross-country travel, they would. But you have to be a member of the club to get the benefits of all they had to offer. We didn't care about the roadside assistance, after all, Jim took the Jeep apart, rebuilt everything, and put it back together. No, we were looking for the famed "Triptik."

The "Triptik" was not just a map with a highlighted route. No, the Triptik provided a personalized travel plan, laid out in a flip-type map with foldouts, put together just for you by a real person that talked to you over the phone. Today you can go to Google Maps, and with the click of a few buttons get the same thing. But back in 1975, the best you could get was a gas station map without all of the details along the way. The AAA information was tested and tried by trusted travelers that rated gas stations, motels, and attractions.

Just to give you an idea of what is in the "Triptik" the first section is "Using your Triptik" and the first paragraph sets the tone for an amazing adventure.

"Your AAA Triptik, a detailed, individually tailored routing is the backbone of the AAA travel package. The clear and informative strip maps answer the needs of today's motorist on today's – and tomorrow's – highways."

Who could resist? The next sections to help with your trip planning needs are;

"Trip Planning and Expenses"

"Driving Tips"

"Speed Limits and Accidents"

"Radio Stations"

"About Accommodations"

And because we were going across the border, into Canada, "Border Regulations."

All this, and the actual flip maps. John thought, how could they make this any better? How about throwing in a couple of Tour Books for Northwestern and North Central USA? No wait, there are more, full-size maps of the areas to be traveled including British Columbia.

There is just one catch... you have to be a member in good standing to receive all these amazing benefits. John's dad was a member in good standing. The only thing in the way was telling him that we were going on a trip the Monday after graduation. Did John forget to tell you that we kept all our planning to ourselves? We didn't want our parents to put the kibosh on what we knew we had to do before we started our lives as real authentic adults.

John made what he knew was a leap of faith and told his dad about our trip, which by now was more than a dream, but a real plan. His Dad was a bit taken aback by how much planning we put into the trip. He jumped on board and made the call to AAA.

Buying the Gear

John and Jim had tons of fun shopping for the best equipment available, from our D3 expedition external framed with new technology hip wings and straps, "Jan Sport" backpacks to our Alpine Designs fiber-filled mummy sleeping bags. According to our research, the fiber-fill was purported to dry easily, and quickly even in sub-zero temperatures, and good to thirty degrees below zero. We also relied on very knowledgeable sales staff that knew all about the products, as they were trained on what the store offered.

Before we had driver licenses and were able to drive, we rode our bikes the three and a half miles to wander the new mall called Randhurst in Prospect Heights. We knew all the stores, especially the backpacking outfitter on the lower level. And when it came time to start shopping, we knew exactly where to go for all our backpacking needs.

Randhurst opened in the middle of 1962. It was not much to look at from the outside. Kinda boxy with the names of the anchor stores displayed at their outside entrances, but it did have a massive white dome in the center that brought to mind a giant flying saucer. When it had its grand opening, John was told there were six ribbons to cut, one for each arcade entrance, as they called them. It was built on one of the last farms in the area and was, at the time, the largest shopping center under one roof in America and possibly the largest shopping center in the world! In its first month of business, more than one million people traveled miles to see this marvel. It was so crowded that you could hardly walk around.

In the late '60s and '70s, Randhurst started to host special events to keep the public interested. Artwork hung in the common areas ranging from modern sculpture to local student drawings, hand-picked by teachers for public display. In 1976 and 1977 they even had a three-ring circus. Because of the uniqueness of the mall, celebrities like Robert F. Kennedy and Arnold Schwarzenegger, just to name a few, also made guest appearances.

The inside was nothing like the boxy outside. When you entered one of the six entrances, your senses were hit with upbeat music, different store signs all lit up, and the smell from some of the shops that sold cookies and fudge. It was also air-conditioned! Today you would expect this in every store you would go in, but back then not many people had conditioned air in their house. So, in the summer this was the place to be.

The building layout was also very unique. Over one million square feet! The outside ring, not a circle, more of a triangle, had the three main anchor stores, Carson Pirie Scott, Montgomery Ward, and Wieboldt's. These anchor stores each had two stories. In between these big three, on the first floor were ninety smaller shops. In the walkways, there were cart vendors or kiosks to catch your eye, a first in America, but have been around since the middle of the 1800s in England where newspapers were sold. Shoppers could rest beside water fountains as the kids climbed on large stone and steel sculptures of horses laying down or penguins. Above these shops, on the mezzanine level were the doctors', dentist's, and professionals' offices. With all the shopping to be done, and a proper temperature of 72 degrees year-round why would you need a coat inside? With that, they even had lockers available to keep your stuff safe while you shop, for a fee of course.

The center of the mall had a clear dome letting in sunlight for all the live plants inside. Under the dome, from the top, down were two restaurants that looked like they were floating on the round second floor. One even had a liquor license and was a fine dining classy restaurant that had great food. Adding to the ambiance it had no ceiling and opened to the dome forming a great airy space. Jim's mother had worked there as a waitress part-time when we were in grade school. She used to bring home leftover Napoleon pastries that were delicious.

You could find about ten shops sunken five steps below the first floor under the floating restaurants. Under that was the lower level or basement that had fifteen smaller stores set in a doughnut style with shops on both sides. On the outside of these shops were the supply tunnels for all the stores. There are rumors that the lower level was a fallout shelter, enough to hold everyone in Mt Prospect at the time of construction. That would be about 11,000 people!

We found all the gear we needed in the equipment stores that peppered the mall, we started at Herman's World of Sporting Goods, and continued to the other major department stores, Ward's, Wieboldt's, and Carson's all that had items on our list. Jim even had some new stitching added to his Fry Boots for $5.00, where the sole was pulling away by the shoe repair guy. He had a little shop in the sunken area in the center of the mall. The distinct waxy smell of greasy shoe polish greeted us as soon as we walked through the door and seemed to linger in our clothes as we left. Jim also picked up some mink oil to rub the boots down with, to make them water-resistant for the trip. We both had previously purchased some leather hiking boots at Kinney's Shoes; the kind with Vibram soles for good grip, to wear while backpacking. Jim liked the high tops to support his skinny ankles. Newer, heavy specialty, insulated hiking boots were available at a hefty price, but we opted for a non-insulated, more of a work boot We felt they afforded us more versatility in the forest. Fry boots were for everything else and were very comfortable once they were broken in.

Count Down

Thirty days before our trip we decided it was time to put this trip into a plan. We knew what we wanted to do but were kind of at a loss on a few details. A big one: what to do with the Jeep while we backpacked. We also had to give the motor club enough time to put this adventure down on paper.

We kind of missed the part about leaving the Jeep in our daily planning sessions. But John's mom was friends with our neighbor Jean across the street. The two women we're talking about our upcoming big adventure. Jean said that her younger brother lived in western Canada, near the west side of the Rockies, in western British Columbia. Without hesitation, John's mom set up a time for us to talk to her and see if maybe something could be worked out about the Jeep.

If this meeting went well, all was good. This huge, and critical piece of the puzzle could finally click into place. If only we handled it right. As we walked across the street, we had no idea what to say or how to ask for her brother's help. After all, what could we offer as a trade to leave the Jeep at his place, for who knows how long?

Now, John grew up across the street from them all his life, but he never met her brother. He was older than us, probably born in the early fifties but probably not as long ago as the forties. So, he must have been about twenty-five or thereabouts. The first thing we thought was he was a draft-dodger because we thought that almost all the young American men who went to Canada at this time were. Why would someone like this help out a couple of kids? Well, there was no turning back. We had to find a way to ask.

Just as we were about to knock on the screen door, it swung open and Jean said "Come on in and have a seat."

She offered us some sweet tea and we listened while she talked. She told us how she heard about our trip and thought it was going to be an amazing adventure. In hindsight, we think she thought we were nuts. But back then no one said it out loud. They just tried to encourage people to try new things. After all, the sixties were not that long ago, and we knew what kind of "adventures" went on then.

After some small talk on the details of the trip, like when we were leaving and about what date we were going to arrive, she excused herself. We thought it was odd that she went into the bedroom and closed the door. So, we just sat there drinking our sweet tea in silence.

It seemed like we waited there for a long time. Five minutes can seem long when you're just waiting and Jean came out and said," It's all set, Stan will be expecting you in the middle of August. He is going to mail you the directions in a few days." She also said if we didn't mind, could we take a care package to him from her. What could we say except sure, and that was that without ever talking to Stan!

John's Prep

As our departure date grew closer, the knot in my stomach was also growing. It was the middle of May. There was still so much to do, and we still needed so much money. I dreaded telling Jim I was short about four hundred dollars. I also did not want to borrow any money for the trip. I was supposed to be saving from the beginning of the school year. Somewhere along the way, my commitment to save gave way to other things I wanted and needed.

One of those things that sidetracked me was something that Jim told me about in the summer of '74; our junior year of high school. He said that one of the gas stations that he did work for was selling a Jeep that they no longer needed. So, on a Friday we drove my 1966 Dodge Coronet 440, which I bought from my mother, across town to take a look at the Jeep. As we got closer to the corner of Wolf and Camp McDonald roads, Jim shouted, "There it is on the corner. "

From a distance, it was hard to make out what it was. There were snowplow parts and tires all around it with the typical service station signs. As we pulled into the parking lot, I was in shock. I was looking at a blue 1967 CJ5 Jeep with a white metal cab and a large yellow rotating emergency light on top. Attached to the front was a yellow two-way plow. The kind of plow that goes up and down, that can also tilt left and right using crude steel hydraulic controls inside the cab. Behind the plow was a sixteen-inch-tall bumper, covered with a heavy layer of rubber that was added by the gas station owners for pushing cars around the lot without scratching them. On the back was another plow that only went up and down, also controlled from inside. This blade was used to back up close to a building, drop the plow, and pull the snow away. This Jeep was a tool for the gas station owners; set up by and heavily used by them daily.

A sign, $2,500.00 firm! Hung in the front window of the Jeep. That was a lot of money. The owner, the guy Jim knew, came out and tossed the keys to Jim and said, "it's got a half a tank of gas and we close at five." (It was 1 pm).

I had never driven a manual transmission before, so Jim hopped in and started it up and said, "Let's go."

He was very familiar with the "stick and clutch," and with Jeeps, for that matter. Off we went for a test drive. Everything was checking out okay. No leaks, nice and tight suspension, tires okay and everything worked including both plows and emergency light. After about an hour driving around, Jim said, where to?" and I said, "Let's go back and talk to the owner".

Like the sign said, $2,500 firm. It was hard to negotiate with that because the Jeep was in pretty good condition. I asked if he would hold it till Monday so I could find the money to pay for it, and he looked at Jim and said, "Sure why not."

After talking to my dad about buying my first vehicle from someone outside of the family, he said he would loan me the money, with interest, just like a bank. He even made up a payment book. This was great because I had no credit, and no bank would loan a kid in high school money. But this did mean Dad would hold the title until it was paid off. Little did I know how this would help me the following year.

Due to the Jeep payments, and all the cost of being a high school senior, the odds of saving were stacked against me coming up with the $400 I was short for our trip. It was a bet not even Jimmy "The Greek" Snyder, the "NFL Today" oddsmaker that reached near folk-hero status until he fell from grace would take.

There just didn't seem to be any extra money to put into the cookie jar. I did have a little money in the savings account, but not the four hundred I needed for our trip. And that money was for emergencies only. I knew all the items we bought were needed, but I was spending a lot more than I should have.

The $ 3.85 per hour I was making at Precise Machine Company was just not going to cut it. Not at a twenty-four-hour workweek. I was lucky to see fifty dollars after Uncle Sam got his cut. Plus, Precise was way over in Rosemont and the expense of traveling to Rosemont, six days a week was enough to break me. I started ride-sharing just like my dad did when I was younger with a friend of mine, Don, who also worked at Precise to cut the cost down. It was still going to take me over two months to save all I needed, and that's without spending a cent on anything.

Then the worst happened. My blue and white 1967 CJ5 Jeep that I bought from the gas station, would not start. There seemed to be something wrong with the starting system. If I gave the voltage regulator a tap with a wrench or tire iron it would sometimes start. Instead of fighting with it this time, I just called the police department to let them know there was a disabled vehicle in the street. That way I would not get a ticket for parking in the street overnight.

About two o'clock in the morning, my dad woke me up and said with a serious grimace on his face that I could barely make out in the dim light "I think you have a small problem to deal with."

I had no idea what he was talking about until I saw my mother looking out the window at her trees in the parkway.

There was now a vacant spot where my Jeep used to be parked. My parents were both awakened by the crash that I had slept through.

My Jeep now rested in the neighbor's driveway across the street. They must have been awake, or the sound was so loud that they called the police right away. When the address of the Jeep's owner was relayed, it was like all-hands-on-deck. You see the Jeep was not registered in my name; it was in my dad's name.

The police were everywhere. Their lights lit up the whole block. There must have been three or four squad cars driving up and down the street looking for the driver and clues to where he went.

It did not take a lot of police work to look for a red vehicle that left red paint all over the rear bumper and heavy rear plow hookup. Or to follow the trail of leaking oil and, a few of his car parts sprinkled on either side of the oil right up to his closed garage door. The dead giveaway was he was still in the driver's seat passed out from a night out on the town.

You might be thinking, how much more bad luck could this guy have? Well, all those police cars driving up and down the street with their lights flashing, and all the officers walking around looking for clues with their flashlights shining like they were searching for an escaped convict. They even brought in the detectives with their unmarked Mercury Marques Interceptor to find the culprit. It sure worked up a lot of attention for such a ruckus. It was not because it was a high-profile crime that was going down. It was because my dad was the police and fire trustee for the village. He was also a Wheeling deputy police officer and a Cook County deputy sheriff. He knew every officer from the years as appointed police and fire commissioner and his now elected position, and they knew him. Plus, it didn't hurt that he was in charge of all promotions within both departments. Not that it would have made a difference, but they all wanted to show that they respected him for the fairness he brought to the positions he held.

I say respected because at this time in Wheeling's history there were quite a few trustees that were under federal investigation for abuse of their position. Mostly the zoning department because the village was growing their industrial section of the area. But there was a deep investigation into my dad's department of unfair promotions or non-promotions. This was due to a few officers who jumped on the bandwagon when they thought they should have been promoted. It turned out that they did not pass the written part of the promotion testing that was kept confidential to protect the officers and it was well documented. When it was to go public my dad asked them if they wanted it to be released. They were pretty embarrassed and declined. He did not hold it against them and they, in turn respected him. It did not fare so well with the others; most went to jail.

By the end of the night, they had their man, and he had a handful of tickets to deal with, and a job well done by all.

Now you might think this is sad. No way. The insurance company had no idea what this thing was worth, so they totaled it. I think the front and rear plow hook-up threw them for a loop. Not only did they give me enough to pay off the outstanding balance to my dad, but I had also enough to buy it back from the insurance company, fix it, and put a thousand dollars in my pocket two weeks before we departed.

There was another thing that had to be done that I was putting off. Letting my employer know I was quitting my job. This was not going to be easy because I had been working for this company for two years and I liked them.

It wasn't the job by any means. It was in a great machine shop. Back then we called it a job shop. That meant we would make parts out of raw metal stock to the customer's specifications. Sometimes it was for a single item. Not too common because of setup costs, and those were usually made by the tool and die, makers. But mostly it was for large batches of parts to be used in making things like slot machines or instrument panels in airplanes. My job was on a milling machine.

All through high school, I was enrolled in the machine shop trade school class. The first two years were learning the basics like ferrous and non-ferrous metals, soldering, and tin work. The machines were for the more advanced junior and senior students. When I picked out my classes for my junior year, my dad thought it would be a good idea to sign up for the work program class. This was great for a few reasons. For starters, the teacher would help prepare me for interviews. They would help me find a job in the field I planned to get into. And the best part, I got out of school early to go to work! On the first day of class, who do I see sitting in the back row? Jim. It was rare in our school to have a class with a friend due to the high number of students.

Once the classroom door closed things started to go downhill fast. For starters, our teacher stood up in front of the class and introduced himself as JW Griffin. With about a five Mississippi pause. Then he held up a wooden pencil about two inches long with an unused eraser on the end and said, "I never make mistakes." With that, Jim and I burst out laughing and the rest of the class joined in. JW assessed the situation and decided the best course of action was to kick Jim and me out and told us to go to the library on the first floor.

I was a little in shock because we were only five minutes into class. But Jim said not to worry, he doesn't like me and kicks me out all the time. But, sent to the library? What are we going to do there? He said follow me. As we signed in and answered the librarian's questions like, why are you late? And who sent you? She understood because JW does this to someone in every one of his classes. She thinks it is his way of controlling the class. Well, whatever. Now what. Follow me, Jim said, and off we went to the back corner, outside wall. Jim unlatched the window's two lever locks, pushed the window open and went through the opening like nothing, and said come on let's go to lunch!

The next day, was like nothing had ever happened and he sent someone else to the library. He didn't seem to hold a grudge and he did set up an interview in Rosemont at Precise Machine Company for me.

I got the job and they put me on an "NC" (numerical control) milling machine. This is an automated machine that can cut metal secured on a bed that moves left and right, in and out, and up and down. The tools could also change as programmed. Back then the program was on a paper tape with perforations, read by air going through the holes. Today they have "CNC" which is computer numerical control. Because I picked up on this machine, they also set me up working an "NC" lathe.

With these new skills who wouldn't be happy to show my shop teacher what I could do? The next day he had me teaching the class. From that point on it was straight A's and never took a test again!

Precise Machine Company was an awesome company to work for. All family in the office, long-term tool and die makers from Poland, and there were only three of us on production. The T&D guys knew their stuff and they were always calling me over to show me how to do something new. These guys were old school, no shortcuts here.

But the crazy thing was, and I don't know if it was because these people worked together so long or their German background. On payday, we would stop working (still on the clock) one hour before quitting time and put a bunch of tables together, pull out a case of beer in quart bottles, a couple of loaves of rye bread with sliced meats and cheeses and play cards till quitting time. This way, none of the employees who were not family got in trouble for going to the bar after work and blowing their paycheck before getting home. No one was the wiser. It kind of makes sense in an old-world kind of way.

But the time to quit finally came. I went up to the boss and told him that I had to quit and the reason why. He said "Good, I am happy that it is not because you are unhappy here. When you are done come back."

And that was that.

Everything was falling into place; we had our common to-do list and our individual lists. For some reason (I always put things off till the last minute) I still needed to get new glasses before we took off because mine got damaged. The optometrist was unsure how long it would take but assured me they would be ready at least a week before the trip. Well, that was a relief until I got the call, they were ready. I did not want to put this off any longer so, off I went right after I hung up. These were a new type for me that would change from clear to sunglasses depending on how bright the light is.

When I put them on, the doctor was looking over the prescription. Then he said what you never want a doctor to say, "uh-oh." Followed by, "They forgot to put the coating on! I can do it here in the office but it takes a few days to do." I could feel a pain in my chest growing just thinking about trying to go on this trip without them. And I think he could see it in my eyes, no pun intended. Luckily, I got them the afternoon before we were scheduled to leave.

Jim's Prep

I had several jobs through high school, as part of the work program. I worked for Bob's Pizza Place, run by Bob and his wife. Bob was a stocky guy with a lot of energy and was a good boss.

Bob's Pizza Place, was in a strip mall, across the street from the high school, sandwiched between "Mark drug store" where my older brother Rick worked, and Ron's Head shop. (Ron was amazing as he knew and remembered the name of every person that ever went into his store. My wife and I went into Ron's store 10 years after our last visit, back while we were in high school, and he knew both our names first and last and we had only been in there a couple of times).

When I was hungry at work, I would ask Bob about different sandwich combinations like "would a beef sandwich taste better on garlic bread," and he would tell me to put one together and try it. The food was always great. Bob's wife ran the dining room and served drinks, she had a less than cheery disposition and rarely talked to the help. Bob was the only one allowed to make pizzas and they were delicious.

Between working at Bob's and my practice for the cross-country team, I mowed grass for Mr. Hursh a co-worker of my mother's. Mr. Hursh had a brick ranch with a half-acre yard along busy East Camp McDonald Road across from Rob Roy Golf Course in Prospect Heights.

As I mowed his lawn, I would admire three Willys CJ2A Jeep's that had been left in the golf club maintenance yard across the street next to an old, dilapidated barn leftover from when the golf course was farmland. Willys-Overland Corp. had manufactured the first Jeeps during WWII and continued to make them until they were sold to Kaiser, then AMC, and they were eventually purchased by Chrysler.

The three Jeeps needed significant repair because, in part, they were sitting for some time with the hoods off and engines disassembled and exposed to the weather. Weeds nearly engulfed them, with a small tree coming through one of the Jeep's, engine compartment.

I knew Jeeps pretty well and my first car was a Willys pickup truck that my father had sold me when I was 14 after he had made a frustrating attempt to drive it to our summer cottage in Michigan, and a significant loss of oil made him turn back. (A cloud of blue smoke as he burnt a quart of oil every 5 miles will do that to a guy). My father had obtained it from the local park district after its retirement from service, like a junkyard rescue. I purchased it from my father for $5.00, that is how frustrated he was.

I pulled the engine, as I had seen my dad do with our Rambler wagon, and with the help of a Motor's Auto Repair Manual, I got from the library, and a little advice from the machinist at the oldest auto shop in town, Wheeling Dunhurst Auto parts, and machine shop. He had worked on these engines during WWII and would like to see them run again.

The engine in the truck was the famous "Go Devil" 134 cubic inch engine used in the military jeeps during the war, it had 60 horsepower and an incredible, 105-foot lbs. of torque.

After nearly a year of mechanical restoration, I learned to drive it in the driveway because at 15 years old, I did not have a driver's license yet. One evening Dad told me I could pull it into the driveway from where it was parked in the street. I was very excited and a bit cocky. I accelerated a bit too much and then confused the brake for the clutch and my dad yelled "slow down," as I raced past him standing alongside the driveway. I did not quite get it stopped before it muscled through the garage door. I thought my father was going to kill me, but as I looked up at the garage door crumpled on the hood, I glanced at the mirror to see my father behind me, doubled over laughing. He and I spent the next weekend building and installing a new door.

One Saturday morning when I arrived to mow his lawn, Mr. Hursh, came out to meet me. He told me he had a surprise for me. He had a few drinks the night before with the owner of Rob-Roy golf course, and he told him of my interest in the old Jeeps. I had always wanted a little jeep 4X4 and admired those CJ2's from afar.

The golf course owner told him that I was welcome to all three of them if I could haul them away. I was ecstatic. As soon as I finished with the lawn, I went directly to our friend Cliff's house, as he had a crazy neighbor, Bob, that owned a flatbed truck for his race car.

As kids, Bob was a constant source of entertainment for us. He was always doing things that made us wonder about his sanity, things like, when he got a dent in his car, he would cut it out with a torch, turn it around and weld it back on making it a bump instead.

When we were in elementary school, we had a clubhouse in Cliff's back yard, and when we spent the night in the clubhouse, we would use Bob's rhubarb patch behind his dilapidated garage to relieve ourselves at night. One year he had the biggest crop ever, and his mother, whom he lived with, made a large number of rhubarb pies. We laughed at the potential of our contribution to the crop and the pies. For this, and innumerable other strange observations growing up, we always just considered him crazy.

Cliff and I went over and found Bob in the garage, I offered him $50.00 to winch the Jeeps onto his flatbed and to deliver it to my house. He quickly rolled his race stock car off the flatbed into his unkempt backyard. The flatbed rumbled to a smoky, smelly start, and Cliff and I jumped into Cliff's mom's Chevy Vega, and the crazy neighbor Bob began to follow in his flatbed truck belching smoke at each shift Bob made.

We drove the four miles or so to the Rob Roy maintenance yard and immediately began to assess the job. It was apparent that we would need to make two trips as we could only fit two jeeps on the flatbed at one time and it was very precarious at that. We loaded the first, then the second. Alongside the Jeep was an old plow that came with one of them, so we muscled that onto the side of the bed.

It was a beautiful day, and we were in great spirits when we got to my house with the first load. As the truck stopped in front of the house with its rusty cargo several of the neighbor's came out to see why a junk truck had stopped in the street in front of our house. We started to unload. We had the first one unloaded and the second half off when my father came out and asked, "What the hell are you doing?" I told him in my excitement that I had acquired the Jeeps and was going get one in tip-top condition.

My father turned red with anger at the massive amount of rusty junk that I had just dumped on his neat, clean, well-organized suburban yard and driveway. Rather than have a showdown right then and there he just shook his head and went back inside. We continued to unload the Jeeps, pushing them up the driveway on flat tires with my pickup truck, while chunks of rust and golf balls fell out along the way. After the second trip, I paid off crazy neighbor Bob, the $50.00 I promised. Even though it took two trips Bob was very happy with the cash.

Once we had them lined up in the back of the driveway up to the garage door, I started to take stock on what I had, trying to determine what Jeep would be the keeper and what would be parted out. Cliff assisted me in this review, and I offered him any leftover parts from my build. We thought we might be able to pull together two jeeps from this three-jeep pile of rusty gold.

I immediately began to tear them down and identify the best components for my build, moving them into the garage.

My family has always been cursed with never being able to park a running car in the garage due to the stuff always piled in there to support our hobby projects. The pungent varnish smell of stale gas and differential grease soon replaced the freshly cut wood of Dad's woodworking space.

After picking out the parts I began to develop a plan of attack. First, tear down the motor to identify the sizes of rings and bearings I needed to order. After that, I could turn my attention to the body repairs.

I noticed many small dents all over the body and it told the story of how this Jeep must have spent quite a bit of time collecting balls on the driving range. I decided to ignore those and address the large rust hole under the passenger seat.

My friend Dan, who lived up the street had been working on a '47 Ford that he was turning into a hot rod. He rented a large air compressor on a trailer with a sandblasting rig. After Dan finished blasting his '47, I brought my Jeep body up the street to his house. With some sharing of the sand, I blasted the body clean of paint and rust.

I cut and fit a steel Century 21 real estate sign over the hole in the passenger side and screwed it in place. I identified a hole in the gas tank and filled it with water, pulled out my Sears oxy-acetylene torch to attempt a braze. To my surprise, a muffled boom startled me, even though I had at most, a bubble or two of gasoline vapors left in the tank. After the adrenaline from the small blast subsided, I was able to braze it to patch it up.

I brought the old crankshaft to Dunhurst Auto parts. As I expected, the machinist knew all the tricks to clean up the shaft and matching the bearings and seals, as he was the same machinist that helped me with the Pickup truck years before. Once the driveline was installed, I painted the body with a Rust-Oleum in a spray can and undercoated the body the same way. One item I do regret was the windshield, the window frame had a piece of flat steel welded around the inside to hold the glass as the original hinged frame was gone. The steel was welded with a bit of a curve that was impossible to fit glass to, so I simply used plexiglass instead. This decision I would later regret, as the slightest rub would scratch the plexiglass and make it harder to see through.

I had all my friends over, kicked up the music in the garage with Grand Funk Railroad playing on the beat-up Bon Sonic 8-track AM/FM radio on the bench, while we got around the body and lifted the body four feet to get it high enough to clear everything including the shift stick and set it onto the frame.

The rest of the summer was spent adding accessories like a new roll bar, and a Panasonic am/FM/weather band cassette deck. I spent a lot of time testing the off-road capability, as we had a few favorite places, and nicknames for all of them. There was a hundred acres or so just north of Wheeling that was an overgrown, abandoned nursery we called 10 Hills for the 10 mounds of dirt someone put in the entrance path to keep people out. On many occasions, we went to a large field that was along Palatine Road that we called "Eat at Joe's" because there was an old billboard that was falling that had the words on it fading from the weather. We would look for any place we could drive off-road that the police wouldn't kick us out of.

I remember on one particular outing at "Eat at Joe's," One guy's Jeep that was only two-wheel drive, was stuck in the mud up to his axel's It was a surplus Mail Jeep he got at a government auction. All the newer CJ5 Jeep rigs with four-wheel drive, and giant mud tires, failed to budge him. I backed my little old 1948 Jeep with its narrow old non-directional military tires up to the mired in Jeep, connected the tow rope, dropped the transfer case in granny low, and began pulling. The stuck Jeep came up and out as my little tires dug in and flew mud out of the tread on each revolution. I'm sure I didn't crow too loudly at my success.

My parents gave me a choice for a graduation present, the same as they had my older brother two years before He had selected an aqua blue fiberglass canoe. I on the other hand needed money for the trip. I was only able to save about $150.00 because I spent all the money that I was able to make at the Autopart's store on parts for the jeep and camping gear. John and I had agreed on $500.00 each, so my parents gave me $350.00 in cash as my graduation gift. This was no insignificant amount for my parents to afford and I was very grateful.

Preparing the Jeep

In preparation for the trip, Jim decided to repaint the jeep that had been originally painted tan with rattle cans, to traffic yellow, with a brush to make sure it had a good protective coat and then added a black canvas top. The Jeep looked good and with a fresh tune-up and a basket of spare parts thrown into the big Craftsman toolbox, it was ready to be loaded.

We did our calculations. The jeep had a fifteen-gallon gas tank, per the book. We strapped on two five-gallon jerry cans to the back of the Jeep. This gave us twenty-five gallons of gas. We seemed to average somewhere in the neighborhood of 23.6 miles per gallon, which gave us a range of five hundred and ninety miles between fill-ups. With an average speed of thirty-two miles per hour, we could travel for almost eighteen and a half hours between fill-ups. That would be nonstop, no breaks except to stop and dump a Jerry can into the tank twice and to empty our own tanks. We did not use the Jerry cans all the time so without the extra on the back, it would be more like a range of 354 miles per tank, in an eleven-hour day.

We fastened a "come-a-long" winch that was mostly used to stretch chain link fence, to the front bumper of the Jeep, as power winches were too expensive, and the "come-a-long" had served us well for many off-road outings. The best part was it was small enough to fit in our limited storage space. With coiled cable and all the power of a hand ratchet, packed into a five-inch by five-inch by a foot-and-a-half long package that with a small pully could pull the jeep out of almost any hole it got stuck in. There was only one catch, it had to be secured to something strong enough that would not pull out of the ground. The Jeep now passed all the checks and double-checks that we threw at it to ensure it was as reliable as possible.

Jim built a wooden counsel box to put between the seats, that held some cassette tapes and misc. stuff, like a knife and registration, cigarettes, and matches. He stained and coated it with varnish for weather protection. He added a key lock, just in case we wanted to store valuables.

Jim also built a bench seat in the back that was a little more than what it appeared to be. It was made out of three-quarter-inch plywood with a hinged top and a nice heavy-duty padlock mounted in the middle. The top had a four-inch cushion with a black Naugahyde cover on it that matched the front seats during his original remake. It turned out to be very comfortable to sit on despite not having a backrest. Keep in mind that this was the seventies so there were no seat belts installed. When you lifted the bench, you could see ample room inside alongside two, nine-inch Jensen triaxial speakers mounted on the inside front. Jim surrounded the speakers with wood to protect them from damage, which also helped with the sound quality; not that the Jensen's needed help. On the outside, the speaker holes were covered with the factory black grill that also matched the seats. What you did not see was the hidden compartment on the bottom front of the bench.

Jim created a clever, almost invisible drawer in the bench below the speakers. It could only hold something four inches tall but wide enough to go from wheel-well to wheel-well. Because the Jeep had a soft top that could not be locked, we needed a secret compartment with no-lock fast access. This was where we kept our rifles and shotgun: perfectly fitted for one 303 British Enfield, one 22 caliber rifle, and one 12-gauge break-down shotgun with room to spare for another rifle and enough ammunition for anything our imaginations conjured up.

Buying the Food

Because of our extensive Boy Scout training, we thought we knew everything there was to know about shopping for food. After all, both of us survived numerous campouts, and we had some of the best scout leaders any scout troop could ask for. We had packed for two, and three-day weekend trips all the time. We completed the required tasks to have earned our cooking merit badge and received our cards, and we were first class scouts. We were even with the US Air Force when they were doing their training for survival on one occasion. That's where we learned how to eat the root of the cattail plant and use the dandelion leaves for a salad if we had to for survival. They also told us to not eat anything that we were not 100 percent sure was okay.

When we left for the supermarket that still, June night, bound and determined to succeed with this minor detail called shopping. We knew it was better not to split up, that is unless one of us had to go for help. After all, this was uncharted territory for both of us. The success rate for a completed mission relied on a complete and practical evaluation of our needs. Our wants had to be put to the side, at least for the time being.

On the way to the store, we had some last-minute thoughts. There were a lot of things to consider, for starters, we were going to be gone for a very long time. There was a budget to maintain, along with limited space (not much room in the back of a Jeep). All these factors combined put an extreme amount of pressure on our shoulders. We reviewed our shopping strategy over and over again. You know the kind of things only other shopping veterans talk about, behind closed doors: coupons, the odd taste of the generic brands, and of course, the two-for-one trap. We also knew from our business class how the big stores would put higher-priced items at eye level to catch our attention fast, and so we'd leave the cheaper items behind. With all that knowledge, we believed we were prepared.

The lights of the National Food Store at Dunhurst Plaza called to us like the beacon of a lighthouse calls to the lost ship. It drew us closer and closer to the big glass windows with all the advertisements. Despite our knowledge, we made a rookie mistake; we shopped hungry. We forgot to eat before we left. But, then again, when is a teenage boy not hungry? We never would have guessed what was going to happen when all that food came into sight? There were so much of everything, in all types of inviting packages, and price ranges. And the colors of the packages against the lights were hypnotic, almost luring us into a trance. But the smells of the samples, freshly cooked, in those portable ovens, were too much for us. We had to retreat. We only had $100 allotted for food, and with all that temptation, we knew we'd be lucky to get halfway through the store before we blew our budget. They had us and we knew it. We escaped with our money still in our pockets.

Our second attempt brought us back the next night, more prepared with full stomachs and before dark. We were on a level playing field now. Yes, we saw the strategically placed items on the shelves as our business teacher warned. But with full bellies, the colors and smells seemed muffled, compared to the night before. We were confident of success this time.

Besides, time was running out. If we were going to do this, it had to be done, now, without second thoughts.

Our shopping list contained all canned or dried goods! Not enough variety to sustain life. No meat or fresh vegetables but plenty of baked beans. Fifteen cans to be exact. Total cost without tax $71.58

We spent a lot of time packing all the things we needed. Backpacks on the sides, tied to the roll bar, guns in the secret drawer, and canned goods, with soft items on top. We chained our toolbox to the front of the Jeep. We packed with our checklists beside us, to make sure we had everything.

Our final thing to do was to pull out all our money and count it up and figure how we were going to manage it. We were too young for credit cards, and this was long before debit cards, Venmo or Apple Pay, or any sort of electronic cash that is so common now. John's dad suggested that we should put some or most of our money in Traveler's cheques. We never heard of Traveler's cheques, let alone ever used them. It did sound like a good idea to protect our money in case we were robbed or lost it. So off we went to the bank to find what we had to do.

The teller must have had a slow day because she was asking us all sorts of questions. Why we wanted them, where we were going and how much did we want? It was the look on our faces with the last question that told her we had no idea what we were doing or what we wanted.

After about twenty minutes we decided to put $800.00 in cheques and keep the rest in cash. We'd each hold in half. We got in $10.00 and $20.00 cheques. We thought we did pretty good figuring that part out. Next, we had to learn the rules of engagement. To the uninitiated, Traveler's cheques are not like regular checks. No, these are registered by number, recorded, signed, and need to be counter-signed when used in a transaction.

The bank teller already had them split up in two stacks. She told us that once we signed a cheque only the signer could use it. It also had to be counter-signed in front of the person you were giving it to and the signatures better match! It took another twenty minutes before we tried to leave.

As we started to walk away from the counter the teller said, "Remember, those are in US dollars!" Duh, we know. We just gave it to you. Not thinking about what was to come when we got to Canada.

The Start

We had girlfriends, Jeanann and Debbie, and families to say our farewells to. The girls thought we were nuts, but supportive, and our families were somewhat indifferent. My mother was a bit of a free spirit and traveled on adventures in her past, so she understood our motivation. Jim's father was just happy to get that jeep out of his garage.

We made a promise to call home every week or so. Our parents agreed to let us call "collect." Back when all phone calls were tethered to what is now an almost extinct thing call a landline, calls were either local or long-distance. A local call applied to a specific geographic area and did not incur a charge other than the expected monthly charge. "Long-distance" was a call outside the local range and the charge accrued by the minute. The further away the caller was, the higher the charge. Most people tried to avoid "long-distance" calls and when they did make them, they watched the time carefully. A long-distance call usually meant there was something urgent to talk about.

One way around getting charged for "long-distance" was to call "collect." In this case, the receiver of the call agreed to pay the "long-distance" charge. "Collect" calls required assistance from the Operator (almost always a woman.). The exchange went something like this:

Operator: Operator. May I help you?

Caller: I'd like to make a collect call to 313-555-1212.

Operator: Your name, please.

Caller: Joe Blow

Operator: One moment please while I connect you.

On the other end of the line: Hello?

No respectable person called "Collect" unless he had a downright emergency. Most people that called "Collect" were downright cheapskates, jerks, or cads. Sometimes friends and families would work out a code to avoid any charge at all.

We knew people who worked out a code word such as "Barn-door" and the caller would blurt it out. Or maybe you just needed to be picked up from work, so instead of Joe Blow, you said your name was Joe Work. The code words meant something like, "pick me up from work" or "I arrived safely." The person receiving the call would refuse the call and no charges would be made. A pretty slick workaround. When John told his mother about this master plan, she said she was well aware of this because she was a telephone operator in the early fifty's.

Digital photography was somewhere in the algorithmic thinking of a grad student. We each had our own camera with something called film. John's camera was a point-and-shoot Kodiak Pocket Instamatic 20. His camera used the four bluecoat flashbulbs in one cube that snapped in on the top. Jim's dad saw John's Instamatic and thought we needed a better camera for the lifelong memories we were soon to experience. Jim's was a Minolta SRT 101 35 mm manual focus with through-the–lens exposure metering. It took great pictures and was marketed in 1966 for the "demanding amateur and semiprofessional photographer."

It took a week or more to get the film developed. So, we made arrangements to alternately send the film home to both parents. This way we each would get a copy when we got back. Plus, they got to see where we were even though it could be three or four weeks after the fact.

They could get two copies developed at Kutza Rexall Drugs at Dunhurst Plaza on Dundee and Elmhurst Roads, where we purchased our bulk Sulfur, and Potassium nitrate for our explosive backyard sciences projects when we were younger, or Wolf Camera on Rand Road just north of Dundee Road. The afternoon before we left, as we finished packing the Jeep and planned our early getaway in the morning, Jeanann and Debbie surprised us by stopping by to see if we needed any help packing. They more than likely just wanted to see what we were bringing but, that's okay. It gave us some relaxing time before our anticipated rush to get on the road. After everything was packed and double-checked, all fluids were topped off and a second look for leaks, we did the customary handshake for a job well done.

This was a good time to get something to eat so, we took a few pictures of all of us as couples behind the jeep.

John and Debbie got in his dad's Dodge Coronet 440 that he sold back to his dad after he bought the jeep and, drove over to Golden Bear in Buffalo Grove for a sit-down dinner. This was near where Debbie lived. After sitting and talking for hours (and leaving a good tip) John drove Debbie home.

Jim and Jeanann jumped on his Kawasaki H2 motorcycle and rode up to "The Old Neighborhood" restaurant on Wolf Road for some cheesesteak sandwiches for dinner. It was great to hear the ringing of the big 2 stroke 750 cc engine again. With all the trip preparation, the motorcycle hadn't gotten the early-season attention it deserved. Jim put the bike away and said his goodbyes as Jeanann left.

Cedar Falls, Iowa (John's Story)

On June 6th, Jim pulled up in front of my house at 8:30, in the morning, the Jeep squeaked to a stop at the end of the driveway, right on time, as planned even though we stayed up late saying goodbye to Jeanann and Debbie. It was a beautiful day, in the mid-seventies with a chance of light rain starting just around 11:00 am and predicted the temperature going up in the mid-eighties. There was not much for me to load up, just my pack, since we loaded everything else the day before, packing and repacking until everything fit just right in the jeep. My backpack fit perfectly against the roll bar. Jim's was on the other side. This left the rear seat open and uncluttered. After my parents took a quick picture, we left Wheeling at 8:35 AM.

I got a strange feeling when we pulled away. Seeing my parents standing there in the driveway waving at us until we rounded the corner tugged at something in my chest, which I later interpreted as a realization that my parents were at least a bit worried. They knew there was nothing they could do to stop us, and for us, we saw no obstacle in our path that we could not handle.

The "Triptik" gave us our first heading: west on Dundee Road.

We did not get far out of town when we entered the expressway. Jim was pushing the jeep as hard as he dared as we needed to make the minimum expressway speed of 45 MPH. The low gearing in the jeep (5.38 to 1 differentials) caused the engine to run at a high 3700 RPM to maintain this speed and the high torque "Go Devil" engine was screaming at that RPM.

After 10 miles or so we got pulled over by a state trooper. He was an older chubby man with an impeccable uniform. He was so mad at us for going too slow on _his_ expressway.

He said, "Don't you crazy bastards know you could explode if you are hit from behind with those jerry cans!"

Our guess is he almost hit us when he was flying down the road in his cruiser, and the bright red jerry cans caught his attention at the last second. He also saw us drinking out of our canteens because it got pretty warm in the jeep at high motor RPM. He probably wanted to take a sniff to make sure we weren't drinking anything we shouldn't be. But he didn't.

When the trooper could not find anything to pin on us, he kicked us off _his_ highway. So much for the Triptik directions, we had to improvise until we were out of the trooper's territory. We ended up going west on Grant Highway. We stopped at a "no facility" wayside to eat our freshly made peanut butter and grape jelly sandwich lunch outside of Freeport at 12:30 PM.

PB&J might not sound like a great meal, but to us this was heaven. Fresh white bread and unopened jars of peanut butter and jelly don't get much better. This also gave us a chance to look over the Jeep and make sure everything was working properly before we were too far from home. We had traveled just 98 miles in 4 hours as the Jeep's low gearing kept us moving very slow.

It started to rain at 1:00 pm and lightly rained for the rest of the afternoon and into the early evening. We continued uneventfully west, crossed the Mississippi after Galena into Dubuque. The area approaching the river and immediately after was comprised of hills, valleys, and varying terrain. Past

Dubuque, we traveled through nothing but flat farmland without many features. The ride for the rest of the day was essentially boring with changeless scenery.

The log we decided to keep showed we traveled a total of 277.9 miles the first day, in 10 hours, at an average speed of 27.75 miles per hour. No wonder we got kicked off the highway. We must not have been close to the minimum speed of 45 miles per hour. Jim was thinking the speedometer was not all that accurate with the vibration of the engine at high RPM.

As a bonus with the Triptik, we got a "where to stay" guide. This was great because it told us where all the free camping was. Jim found a small local free campsite in Blackhawk County, Iowa, just outside Cedar Falls. We pulled in for the night in the late afternoon. The campground was more like a small picnic area. It had very few trees with a parking lot more like a wayside.

We pulled the jeep just past the parking area over a slight hill and into a small grassy valley between several small hills. We started to dig out the tent and set up when it started to lightly rain again. We could not help but get wet and uncomfortable, but due to the fatigue of a long slow ride, we did not mind as long as the Dinty Moore Beef Stew was hot. You would think getting a fire started in the rain with wet wood would be our biggest problem. This was our only way of cooking and we did not bring wood with us. With our many years of scouts and our recent survival class to draw upon we used the tricks of the task. Our fire started faster than the tent was set up! The food was so lacking in culinary character, but it was fast, hot, and tasty. To this day we both still like beef stew, maybe not the canned version but stew nevertheless.

Unfortunately, the next morning, we were forced to pack up in a constant drizzle. Breaking camp in the rain is a sad experience. Setting up a wet tent with no hope of drying out is even sadder. On a positive note, the tent did keep us dry... for the most part. Our feet must have found the low spot where we set up and our feet were soaked by morning.

The jeep rumbled to a start and we each checked our campsite area to make sure nothing was left behind and, like the training the Scouts gave us, that the site was in better shape than when we arrived.

As we pulled out on the road, we noticed it was flat and visibility was for miles without other cars to be seen. The heater in the jeep was not that good. Still, in no time at all, it did the trick of drying out our special fiberfill sleeping bags. We purchased these especially for this feature (and the ability to be warm at -30 degrees) So far, the sleeping bags worked as advertised.

Even though the weather was a bit dismal at this point in the journey, it had not dampened our spirits. John and I, now fully rested, looked forward to the next stretch of road ahead, optimistic about how far we would get this day and what we would see.

Stone Park, Iowa

After another long uneventful day of driving through the flat, almost featureless farm fields of Iowa, we came to a campground that seemed to be private but had the honor payment system of the state parks. We quickly found a suitable spot in the neat rows of campsites accessed from the central gravel path just wide enough for a vehicle. The campground looked to be about two-thirds full but was very quiet and everyone was settling in for the night after their day of travel. We were no exception. We cooked some soup and headed for the sleeping bags as the sun set.

We were awakened by muffled sounds, like a large fist pounding on a wooden table. The layer of canvas between us and the outdoors filtered little in the way of sound! The birds could be heard chirping in the distance, along with the wind rustling the tent flaps. Campfire smells from neighboring, campers brought abundant the aroma of frying bacon and egg breakfasts. None of that explained the vaguely familiar sound that woke us.

As we rubbed the sleep out of our eyes, we matched the sound with our experience. At once, the adrenaline started to pump as we tried to get dressed as fast as we could. There was no time for coffee or a smoke and, we didn't even have time to wash. We started to walk like speed walkers in the direction of the sounds. With each turn in the path, the muffled table-tapping became louder, a more distinct crack, and our excitement grew. As we rounded the last curve the sounds grew into sharp cracks, one right after the other! Yes, it was a shooting range!

Somehow, we managed to stay at a local sporting club's overnight spot. There was a place to buy targets, ammunition, and refreshments. So, we bought a target and set it up on the 100-yard range. You know, "when in Rome..."

When we got set up at the range, only two people were still shooting: an older black guy showing his twelve-year-old son how to shoot a twelve gage with slugs on a 50-yard range. We were pretty impressed; he did have a pretty good grouping for being fifty yards away from his target with iron sights.

These two experienced range shooters must have thought we were nuts when we brought out a twenty-two, a 303 British Enfield, and a twelve-gauge pump shotgun. All to shoot one target. And both of us shooting at the same time.

We saved the twelve gauge, with the double 'O' buckshot until last because we knew there would not be anything left of the target after we hit it with that. Or so we thought. We had an excellent group with both the 22 and the 303, but the shotgun did not even hit the target at that distance.

I bet the old man knew it and laughed up his sleeve at us the whole time. So, what? We all had a good time and laughed about it the rest of the morning. After the shooting, John started a fire and cooked some scrambled eggs and toast.

We left the campground a 12:30 PM, later than we planned as we had such a good time at the range and a lingering breakfast.

We stopped for a late lunch at an A&W drive up at 4 PM for a quick bite to eat. After all, we were planning on being on the road for a long time maybe even an all-nighter.

Back home one of John's favorite meals was A&W's Texas Burger Baskets and a Root Beer. You could smell the greasy aroma of the burgers cooking as smoke from the flat top came steaming out of the hood vent on the roof. Two of our friends, Cliff and Dan, worked there. Jim spent a lot of time there, so he did not have a favorite anymore and we just stopped there on my behalf. We did have a few good laughs recalling how the circumstance when Cliff started there, he had to wear the dog costume and walk around for hours at a time in the hot summer. The manager found great pleasure making all the new employees ware it until a new hire took their place.

While we waited for our food, we decided to do some repairs on the Jeep. The top had come loose from the track on top of the windshield. The canvas had a stiffener sewn in that simply pushed into a channel, and with the wind and bouncing that we put it through it began to slip out of the channel. Jim pulled out the tools and using a tongue and groove plier that was known by its brand name "Channel-lock", squeezed the channel to narrow the slot that the top slipped into. That seemed to do the trick and no more trouble was to be had with the canvas top. As we inspected the jeep's drivetrain, we noticed a loose bolt on the front differential near the bottom. It had developed a slow leak so we tightened the easily accessible bolt and were satisfied everything was in good shape.

At last, the car hop skated up with our food. She was a little taken aback by the soft-sided doors and plastic windows. She had nothing to hook the food tray on. It must have been a full thirty seconds before she just handed the tray through the window.

We both enjoyed listening to music, but when we couldn't get a radio station, we would play our cassette tapes, however, our library was quite limited. We were always singing to CCR, "Up Around The Bend" and "Lookin' Out My Back Door". At the next store we stopped at, we asked someone at the counter of the general store, about the same age as us, if they had any "Canned Heat" thinking they would know that band. The attendance replied that the Sterno (jelled alcohol fuel) was in the back. We guessed they only had 2 kinds of music in the store "Country", and "Western."

Through our stops for food and fuel people could tell we were campers. Without asking for it, locals volunteered suggestions on where to stay and what to see along our planned route. By the suggestion of one of these newfound friends, we stopped for the night at Stone State Park just north of Sioux City Iowa, right next to the South Dakota border. We did not look for it in our travel material, we just wrote down the directions as they told them to us and it took us a little farther than we would have liked to get there but, it was nice. It would have been better if we could have taken in some of the amenities they had to offer. For this night, there was not much going on.

Cottonwood Lake State Recreation Area, Nebraska

Once on the road, we began to have a problem with the speedometer needle jumping from 5 mph to 60 mph, so we pulled over and Jim reached under the dash and unscrewed the speedometer drive cable that ran up from the transfer case. We stopped at the next Standard Oil gas station to pick up some differential grease and topped off the differential that was leaking the day before. Tightening the differential cover bolt did the trick, and we had no more trouble with leaking grease. We also picked up some graphite grease which Jim squirted down the speedometer cable housing and reattached the cable to the speedometer, solving the needle jumping problem. The leaking differential gear grease hitting the exhaust system as we drove made the inside of the jeep smell like a junkyard fire. However, once it was repaired, the smell diminished after a few days.

As we traveled West, we had to stop at a Sinclair service station for gas. Just past the green concrete dinosaur statue in front of the station, the changeable steel panel sign said 54.9 cents per gallon a whopping price jump from 1973 when it was 37.0 cents per gallon. That was the gas shortage caused by OPEC. Jim was working at Purple Martin gas station, wearing the company's red jumpsuit and cap during the shortage, and he had seen half a mile lines waiting for gas at the station when it was available. The shortage started in October 1973 and ran about six months. In 1974 it went up 33% another or 13¢ and we were wondering when it would stabilize.

As we drove over the hose that made the bell go dink, dink, the middle-aged attendant came out of the flat-roofed station in coveralls with an oily red shop rag in his hand. We knew he was working on one of the two cars in the two-bay garage from the dirty oil on his coveralls. Jim told him to fill her up and pointed out the window at the gas cap on the driver's side, just below the door because most modern cars had the filler cap under the rear license cap, not under the driver's seat like the Jeep. He gave us a greasy smile, apparently remembering the good old days when he could find the gas cap with no problem.

Gasoline fumes burned at our nose hairs and our eyes teared up. The attendant reached for the windshield with his oily rag, whistling as he continued the routine everyone expected from a full-service gas station. Jim reacted first to stop him; our fear of Plexiglas damage more volatile than the gas fumes. Who knows what all that oil would do, not to mention the possibility of new, deeper, scratches? John took a soft rag, wet it, and lightly wiped the window in one direction to avoid as many scratches as possible. We quickly got in the habit of washing the windshield ourselves with the more water the better. An attendant would inevitably scratch it all up with a dry or dirty rag. The last thing we needed was circular clouds of scratches in the blinding sunshine.

For the first time in a long time, we turned the radio on and found a news channel; kind of a doom and gloom station. We heard various news stories that seemed like omens of impending disaster ahead. The US Geological Survey noted that Mt. St. Helens, a volcano, would most likely erupt in the next decade, Idaho had a 6.5 earthquake and two larger ones occurred in Alaska.

For the most part, not much happened on Day Three. The weather was good, the tunes flowed and the conversation was filled with anticipation of the next events.

We pulled into the Cottonwood Lake State Recreation Area around 8 pm after driving three-quarters of the state of Nebraska. Needless to say, traveling west with or without sunglasses was very hard at times, especially with the plastic window full of micro-scratches, creating a significant glare at sunset despite our attempts to prevent them. As hard as we tried not to scratch that thing, it always showed every flaw when the sun hit it, so glare was inevitable. Although we would have preferred not to, we had to wash it more often at night, as it seemed during night driving the windshield became a bug magnet, especially as we drove through wooded areas that had not been subjected to high concentrations of DDT as the farmlands were. We never would have predicted that Plexiglass is sensitive even to the exoskeletons of insects.

After picking out a campsite from all the possible locations (we were the only ones there on a Wednesday night,) the wind started to pick up. This wasn't a light breeze; this was a steady thirty mile an hour wind that appeared to be growing. We got the site cleared and the tent set up, far from the first try. With both of us wrestling the thing, we finally got it up. The sleeping bags were unpacked next so they would decompress from their storage.

Now it was time to heat some canned goods, and fast. With a couple of nights under our belts, we saved some firewood from each site just in case we needed a quickfire. We did not need much, just a few small pieces to heat the corned beef hash and corn we were going to cook in the cans. With a quick squirt of charcoal lighter fluid, the fire was lit.

Proud of our skills in the heavy wind, we sat down waiting for our dinner. That's when we saw the storm. There was nowhere to hide, we were out in the open and were going to have to take whatever it was going to throw at us. This was big, it consumed the whole western sky as far as we could see. How could we miss a wall of water headed directly at us? Maybe we were just caught up in getting camp set up and dinner on the fire, maybe we thought it was just nighttime darkness rolling in. Whatever, we had a quick decision to make, fight or flight.

The wall hit us with all its furry. We grabbed the cans of food and put them on the floor in the jeep. We pulled the sleeping bags out and just threw them in the back of the jeep along with the tent. Everything was soaked in minutes, including us. The tent would have been ripped from its stakes or blown to the next county if we stayed. We made the right choice. The storm showed no signs of letting up so we decided to get on the road and just drive on to Custer about seven or eight hours away. There was only one thing in our favor, the food was saved and still hot.

Once back on the road, we had some housekeeping to do, drying out all the wet gear. The sleeping bags were the first thing to address. We had the heater screaming on the highest setting, in an effort to clear the fog off the inside of the windows from everything being wet, and dry out our wet sleeping bags and tent, in a small space. This was a long-fought battle and only added to the stress of the moment.

Let's see if we can describe the "stress of the moment" a little better. Let's start from the outside going in. The full force of the high howling winds was pelting us with big raindrops. The sound of the large raindrops and the howling wind hitting the canvas top was almost deafening at times. No one, in their right mind was on the road. Almost everyone took shelter. The water on the windshield was so thick even with the swipe of the wiper was instantly filled in again. It was better not to run them, and just deal with the sheet draining. On the other side of the plexiglass, we had the fog collecting due to all the gear and us being soaked. We used our bandanas to wipe this off, almost constantly. The heater fan was on high and just about on the verge of squealing like a banshee.

Outside the Jeep, the road was almost invisible because of the combination of the darkness and a thick layer of water covering the road. We chose the safest option: driving in the middle of what we thought was a road. To add a little fun to the mix we were driving along the Niobrara River. The only place for drainage in the middle on one of the flattest states in the US. The small culvert running under the road became a river running across its surface and flooding everything. Sometimes the water got so high it flowed in from the floor drains on both sides of the Jeep.

We lost track of the map in our flurry to take cover. But we knew we had a long way to go on Route 20 Beside the only light in the jeep was a dash light to read the gages, that shined down on the driver's right foot so a map would be little help with nighttime navigation.

To add to all the commotion, we had to get at least the sleeping bags dry. If we had to, the tent could dry out while we set up and with us in it. But not the sleeping bags. A seven-foot-long two-and-a-half-foot wide sleeping bag, good to thirty degrees below zero, takes up some space dry let alone wet. The only place that had any heat was upfront in between the seats. This area had about enough room for a one-gallon milk bottle. Let that soak in, no pun intended. Now these, as mentioned earlier, were the newest fiber-filled, fast-drying best weight to comfort bags out on the market. We were testing that statement to the limit. The bags were so wet that the manufacture could have added a sponge-like response to water as a possible side effect to using in the rain. The first step was to wring out the bag by twisting it like a giant soaking wet towel or dishrag. Next was to try and fluff it up a little and then place it in front of the heater with the fan on high turning front to back every five minutes or so. It worked. We got the job done. At the slow rate of about a foot every fifteen minutes or so. We hoped that in three and a half hours, we'd be past the storm and we could try them out.

A few hours later the rain was finely letting up. Now the silence was almost just as bad as the pelting rain, so we tried to find a radio station. We couldn't find a single FM station and very few AM stations. There was one that had the local news about the flash storm that just rolled through. Maybe they were from Chadron or Scottsbluff. But they were talking about how the river was rising and people along its banks should take precautions.

The rain finally stopped, but our nerves were shot. We needed to pull over and get a cup of coffee and some pie. That fixed almost anything. The problem with that idea was there were not a lot of places where we were, at this time of night. So, every time we came upon any lights, we were looking for something open. At one point we had to drive through flooded streets and the water was coming in the drain holes at the bottom of the door openings partially covering the floor.

We found a major street along Rt 20 or Rt 385 before entering South Dakota that was a little higher and away from the river. We stopped at a café on a street on top of a small hill in the center of town. The wide street was lined with one and two-story brick buildings, they looked to be from the 1890s through the 1920s. Other than a few streetlights, the only activity was coming from the café. We breathed a sigh of relief when we walked in because it was very late, almost midnight, and it was the only place open. As we entered, we could not help but notice the high decorative white tin ceilings of the well-lit, carpeted diner. It was large with many white cloth-covered tables. It was very clean and organized for a café.

The only customers were more than a dozen drunk, men who we thought were migrant workers. With about six whole roasted chickens on their long table. They kept ordering more whole roasted chickens. The frazzled single waitress and cashier were trying to keep up with the men's demands but were having trouble understanding them, as the workers spoke Spanish and the waitress didn't. From the look of the 16-foot table, the group had been there eating for some time.

As they finished eating and drinking, they started to leave one at a time until only one or two remained at the table. We knew exactly what they were doing. They were going to walk out without paying, and we did not want to be around when the last one tried to get out. We paid for our pie and coffee and left a nice tip for the waitress and walked out to a dozen minus one leader, who was still at the table. The group was about twenty feet up the hill from the entrance laughing and doing things they might not normally do but drunk is not normal. The jeep was downhill about 300 feet.

We knew if we started to run, we would be in big trouble, so we walked the 300 feet quickly, but not too fast to draw attention. We planned out what we were going to do as we walked. There was not much of a backup plan. Jim knew that the Jeep probably did not have time to cool down, so it would need to be bump started. So, there was no point in wasting a second trying to start it with the starter. My job was to pull out the 303 British Enfield and load it up with the armor-piercing rounds that we knew would stop any vehicle engine with one shot and be ready if necessary.

As soon as they saw we were about ten feet from our vehicle, they started to run toward us yelling like a herd of drunken goats. Jim put the transmission in neutral and adrenalin must have added to our push. We bump-started the Jeep plenty of times back home. But never with a dozen drunken men chasing us. Jim pushed the clutch in and slammed the trans into third gear before even putting the key in the ignition. It had to be rolling at least five or so miles per hour for the bump-start to work and that was in third gear. John got the rifle out of the secret compartment under the back seat and slammed the loaded clip in and chambered a round. He pointed it out the back window as Jim popped the clutch. The Jeep started, Jim downshifted into second, and off we went. Do you know that feeling that you are being followed? Well, we were looking behind us for the next few hours.

Custer, South Dakota

We pulled an all-nighter just to get to South Dakota and Jim was spent from what we just went through, we switched drivers so he could get some sleep. John felt confident the gallon of coffee he had at the diner, plus the tension from co-piloting during the monsoon had his nerves in the fully awake and upright position. Besides they just needed to stay on Highway 28 and go west till we hit 385. After about an hour, we traveled along in silence. We were out of range of any radio signals and fumbling around in the dark for tapes seemed like suicide.

Every so often, in the distance, a small light flickered in the darkness, and then it was gone. A few minutes later, another flickered. After a little while, the lights were closer to the road and it became obvious, they were oil wells. The light flickering was the flame on top of the vent pipe burning off some fuel. It was starting to turn into a regular, almost timed attraction, giving the driver, John, something he looked forward to. As we passed some that were close to the road the smell of burnt fumes filled the Jeep, and at times a well seemed so close we could almost feel the heat of the fire as passed by.

John's eyes slowly starting to close, so he sat up fast, shook his head, and adjusted in his seat. That fixed things for a few minutes but after a while, the rumbling of all the stuff in the jeep and the humming of the non-directional tires got to him.

He gave one last nod and failed the shakeup. They say if you <u>survive</u> falling asleep at the wheel you will never fall asleep again.

We were going a little over thirty miles per hour, in the early morning hours when John fell asleep. Neither of us felt the jeep drift off the road and drive on the shoulder if that's what happened. No one knows if he swerved into the other lane. What we can say with certainty is that we were the only ones on the road for a very long time. The Jeep went off the right side of the road and down a twenty-two-degree angle slope. It was that sudden shift in angles that startled John into action. He pulled hard to the left and we went uphill and jumped back on the road. We might have been a little air born when we hit the asphalt. It probably didn't take more than a second.

Still, on the same track and speed, Jim lifted his head and said, "You want me to drive for a while?"

"No, I'm good for a little while," said John, his heart pounded in his chest and his eyes were as big as tennis balls.

Jim went back to sleep. About fifteen minutes later John's heart slowed. His eyes grew heavy and his head nodded, so he pulled over and got out to stretch his legs. When he got back to the Jeep, Jim was in the driver's seat.

"I needed that, I will drive for a while," he said.

Jim decided that we should put on some music instead of the dead silence, his choice was, Golden Earring, *Moontan* "Radar Love", very appropriate.

We drove for what seemed like two days straight, we were exhausted from trying to outrun the storm, when we came into the Custer South Dakota area. We thought we pulled off the road, but it was more like just stopping in the middle.

Our task at hand was to find a campground. At this time of night or should we say morning. It was 4:30 am to be exact. We thought it might be better to just sleep in the Jeep. The tall pines just seemed to block any light until the sun was fully visible. Then in the morning sun, we would be able to find a site when the single-day campers packed up and moved on to their next site. By then, we'd have the pick of campsites. Otherwise, we would have to take the most undesirable sites, like the ones next to the garbage cans, or the public pit-style outhouses. So, for now, we just wanted to find a place to sleep. We knew that sleeping on the side of the road was not allowed because we saw signs posted at all the best locations you could pull over to sleep. So, the spot we picked out would have to be off the main highway, and out of sight of the park rangers, or state police.

Somehow, we both knew this area was going to be special, very special, something to remember. You see this was one of our first opportunities where we had a choice of what to do. Up to this time, we were following the AAA Triptik guide. The weather was perfect for a late June night. The sky was clear, and we had no idea where we were.

We saw a sign off to the side of the road that said Lookout Point, and an arrow pointing to a narrow gravel road with mature pines on both sides. We are both suckers for an adventure, and we had no place to be at that moment! So off we went. Who knows maybe there would be a place to sleep at the top?

As we drove up the road, we were hoping this was going to be worth the sharp curves and steep drop-offs that were starting to become more apparent. The Jeep started to show the telltale signs of high-altitude driving: the engine was losing power and it began to sputter as we gave it more throttle. We slowed down and downshifted until we were down to first gear! As we were starting to think that we might be on a road to nowhere, the trees started to thin out. The curves were getting more frequent, and at one point it was like we were going in circles. Just as fast as the curves were coming at us, the road ended and we were stopped in the middle of a small parking lot.

In front of us was a small shack that might have been a lookout post at some time or other. The kind they use for fire watch. The old and weathered wood looked like it could have come off some local barn. The roof, a rust-toned type of metal, appeared to still be working at the moment, but its days were numbered. We could see two signs by the one small light bulb attached to the right side of the building that said Harney Peak el. 7242 and a small arrow pointing to the lookout point behind the building and the other one said "No overnight parking."

We climbed out of the Jeep and started to walk down the stone path. We both looked at each other at the same time; with what would turn out to be the same thought in our minds, but we said nothing to each other. In just a few steps we were there.

A pay telescope in a small semi-circle pointed into the pitch-black abyss that is associated with that time of night. We couldn't see a thing into the valley below, but, when we looked up, we saw more stars than numbers could count. It's hard to tell if it was the elevation or just being on the highest peak in South Dakota, but the stars seemed to want to jump right at us. Almost like wearing Three-D glasses. We realized how at home in the Chicagoland area there is an umbrella of city light that prevents anyone from seeing the true beauty that is hidden behind that curtain of light.

Like most things that happen in our lives, there are many ways to look at things. Some people might have been let down by the lack of view, or the time we wasted traveling such a long way to see nothing. But we took pictures with our minds that no camera could capture. We silently accepted the gift we had at this moment and were humbled by what we had experienced. With that, it was time to move on.

As we pulled out of the parking lot and onto the road leading to our descent, we got a cheap thrill by coasting with the transmission in neutral. If you have ever driven through a mountainous region, you might remember seeing signs reminding you to stay in a lower gear, or not to shift on steep downgrades. We didn't have the safety of runaway ramps if our brakes burn out from overuse. As our speed started to increase so did our inability to control the Jeep. The gravel road was not holding up to the sharp turns that the Jeep's tires were demanding. We were dangerously close to sliding off the edge of the road. Our hearts pounded; each turn felt like a triumph over Death. Time raced by at a frantic pace. Like waiting in line for the roller coaster ride/ impatience turned minutes into hours., In a split second, it was over; we were at the highway turnoff for the Lookout Point. We felt awaken, refreshed, and exhausted!

The exhilaration faded fast. At that time of night, and in our condition, we could hardly focus on driving. Even reading a map didn't seem to make any sense anymore. All that was left was to laugh at the situation. Some people might have started to panic at the lack of control we had. We thought we were aware of our surroundings. We had plenty of food and water, and the cigarettes just seemed to keep us going.

Neither of us could remember the last time a car passed us on the highway. Except for the sign to Lookout Point, there wasn't another sign in sight. It was just as dark at the base of the mountain as it was at Lookout Point. Sometimes the trees would arch over the road and make it appear even darker. We knew where we came from, there was nothing behind us. The only choice we had was to keep going in the direction we'd chosen.

At a small curve in the road, we saw what looked like a gravel shoulder. It appeared like the perfect spot to sleep for the night. The trees near the back edge of the shoulder seemed to give it a canopy effect. This gave us a sense of shelter and provided the perfect place to sleep for the rest of the night, without being ticketed by the police. After all, we saw no signs anywhere, most notably, none that forbid overnight parking.

We filled the back area of the Jeep almost to the point of overflowing with the unpacked sleeping bags and tent. Jim came up with a smart idea during the Jeep re-make, he did not tighten the nut holding the steering wheel in place. It was still safe, there was a cap that prevented the nut from coming off the spindle. This allowed us to take the wheel off and stretch out as much as possible for some shut-eye.

It could have been thirty or sixty minutes. We were out cold. The lights shining in our eyes, and then tapping on the hood, woke us like a poke in the ribs with a sharp stick! Jim sat up, with the steering wheel loose in his hands. John grabbed a map.

The Troopers asked if we needed help. Jim said we were lost, that way, maybe, they would not send us on our way. As the lights scanned the inside of the jeep, we could instantly see our mistakes. The map John was holding was upside down, and the steering wheel Jim was holding was nowhere near the steering column.

We knew that Troopers, in general, trying to protect us and look out for the safety of the masses. But their giggling did not need to be accompanied by words. They knew we were busted, and we knew it too. So, it was up to us to break the silence.

We asked if they knew where a campground was that might have empty sites. They said the State Park was full, but the National Park might have a few open sites. We said great, could they steer us in the general direction of the campground. They said there's no need to, we were parked in the middle of the road leading into the campground.

The thought of sleeping next to an outdoor pit toilet or garbage can does not excite us but finding a campsite in the middle of the night would. The odds were not in our favor at this hour but, we would never know unless we tried. After all, we knew the Troopers were probable still nearby and talking to all their buddies on their radios about the kids in the little yellow Jeep.

As we drove over the cattle crossing (about twenty, two-inch galvanized pipes laid in a cement box) at the entrance to the camp, we wondered why they needed the protection. There didn't seem to be a need to protect anyone from cows. The last time we saw any cows were back in Nebraska. The thought of buffalo never crossed our minds; neither did the notion of keeping animals contained within the park!

On we went through the narrow winding roads of the campground. Our fears soon became reality. Even the undesirable sites were already taken, and we were just about at the end of the loop in the campground. We figured we had two choices: take our chances out on the road, or drive through the campground again. We opted for the latter because we saw that the Troopers were still sitting in the same spot we left.

It was dark and late at night, and we had to drive through the campground in first gear and with just the running lights on. This is the proper etiquette for late arrivals so as not to disturb the other campers when as we looked for a campsite or while setting up. This could be grounds for a complaint to be filed, and we knew the complaint department was at the front door.

So off we went again, headlights off, and in first gear. Every time we thought there was an empty site, on went the lights. At this point we did not care, we were desperate. We developed a new respect for the one-lane road going through the campground when we pulled the lights on. You might think this is an odd term but the light switch is a pull-type two-position switch. With a short pull the running lights would turn on and the dash lights could be dimmed as needed by turning the knob.

When pulled all the way out the headlights would come on. If you wanted to turn on the high beams there was a floor switch that you would step on to turn them on and off. Every time we changed the empty darkness to a small bit of illumination, we could see the sides of the road and just past that the very steep drop-offs. This kind of shocked us a little because a National Campground is supposed to be made safe for all.

In about the middle of the park was a sharp curve to the right creating a loop ending with a steep incline, about five or six feet above the road line. Jim backed up and found a small brush-lined path heading up the slope. With the curve of the road, the Jeep's running lights didn't shine on the path, and we missed it the first time through the park. This needed further exploration.

Out came the flashlights, and up we walked. It was an empty site! Because of the odd path leading to it, all the other campers must have missed it or passed on it. We even had a hard time driving up the path. It had all the amenities of a proper campsite, a picnic table, and a flat spot just large enough for our tent.

The next order of business was to set up a quick camp without waking up the whole campground. Our tent was as simple as it gets. We purchased it from K-Mart for the trip. It was bright orange nylon with a blue nylon floor, it had sides that went up on either side about 14 inches with three string-anchored points to hold out the pitch of the roof, a pole on each end, similar to a pup tent. It had that nylon smell with a hint of mildew stink from the times we had to pack up wet. We got it up in no time. We laid the sleeping bags just before our body's hit the ground, and we were out like lights.

Simmering coffee woke us up earlier than usual. The aroma of nearby campfires brewing coffee tempted our subconscious. We were like that mouse in a Tom and Jerry cartoon; following a tempting aroma without any willpower. We knew this was normal for the "sunrise campers." They get up first and hit the road. They're the type that must be at the new campsite and set up before dinner. Even though we didn't get much sleep, we knew by the number of cars and trucks moving around the campground, there were going to be a lot of empty sites before the morning ended.

The early morning sun was just starting to warm the inside of the tent to an uncomfortable temperature. Anyone who has been camping in the summer knows this feeling. Let's say hot with no airflow. If there was one thing that was going to get us out of the tent that early in the morning, it was going to be the heat. As we were getting ready, we knew the tent had to be shaded if we stayed... If nothing else, we knew how to quickly learn from our mistakes and we were not by any means early risers.

A very bright paradise magically appeared before our eyes the moment we unzipped the tent and popped our heads out. A new adventure was in every direction. Our eyes were still glazed over from the previous night's experience, but the juices were now flowing. The only thing we needed now was some coffee and tunes.

Our campsite perched us at one of the highest points in the park. Our tape of *Credence Clearwater Revival*, "The Midnight Special," ripped through the air. It might not have been the most neighborly thing to do, but so what. We were quiet during the night. Now it was our turn to unwind. Besides, very few of the people around us were going to stay another night.

We could see directly below us the road that serpentines through the campground, and the campsites that we passed in the night. Now, along with the beauty of the area were bewildered faces looking in our direction, recognizing that somehow, we snuck upon them in the middle of the night invading their space. The space they thought was probably uninhabitable by normal people, like themselves. We were what they were trying to get away from teenagers. Now we were their neighbors, like it or not.

We got the fire going in no time, due to all the small sticks all around the campsite. It was almost as if someone had just shaken the trees the night before just for us. At that moment, how they got there didn't matter. Neither of us wanted to go very far this early in the morning. The music helped, but we depended on the coffee. The fire roared with the sound of crackling pine, and a mixture of campfire smoke, pine trees, coffee-filled our lungs. This would have made a great TV commercial with their spokesman, Mrs. Olson, saying Folgers's coffee, it's the richest kind, in her Swedish accent.

The coffee went down smooth and quickly. We had two pots, the small quick one and the larger evening one. Breakfast usually called for the smaller one of the two, but today the larger one fits the need. As our heads started to clear up, we saw that the shade from the trees pointed to the spot the tent needed to be. This would be the first order of business after breakfast. Our choices for breakfast were usually, oatmeal or pancake, today appeared to be a less involved oatmeal day.

During breakfast, we decided this place needed further exploration. At that moment we were not sure if it was the place, or just the time in our lives, that needed the exploring. At any rate, we were in no hurry to be anywhere but right where we were.

The view sure helped; it was spectacular. Even the view of the pit toilets about a hundred yards behind us seemed to blend in. They looked like split logs cut from the same pine trees that were all around us. Because they were just far enough away and slightly uphill, we didn't get the typical pungent, weeks old, built-up, unflushed toilet smell at all. Instead, we just sucked in the strong smell of the Ponderosa pines. Besides, those pit toilets were probably the cleanest we'd had ever seen or used. It was almost a joy to be so close.

Later on, we realized everyone had to come near our camp sooner or later. A lot of people would nod hello if we made eye contact. Some would stop and strike up a conversation. These were the ones that accepted our music and our age. Some of them would even turn into our friends.

After breakfast, we took a quick drive around the park to find a more suitable campsite. It appeared, by sheer luck, the site we were forced to take the night before, was good. Granted it wasn't the best site in the park, but we did not have to move. We did however need to pay each day. The two dollars per day sure was a real bargain compared with some other campgrounds.

So, we moved the tent into the spot that had the most morning shade, and the fact that it was on a high point in the site helped with rain deflection. This would prove to be a real benefit in the days to come. The morning sun, during this time of year, could make the inside of the tent about twenty degrees warmer than the outside temperature. Since we were not exactly the morning kind of guys, this would give us a couple of extra hours of sleep.

All the gear was still damp from the storm we were caught in before we arrived. The rope from our survival kits made a perfect clothesline, which proved to be one of the only times we would use any part of our survival kits or training. The clothes, packs, and bags needed some well-deserved air. Even though there is a kind of camping etiquette to minimize clothesline use amongst campers, we felt a short violation would be forgiven.

The inside of the Jeep needed a good cleaning also. After all, if this was going to be home for a few days, we might as well do a clean sweep and do it right.

The camp looked like hell with all the clothes hanging around and the stuff from the jeep scattered in all directions. But the sun was doing its job, and time was the only thing that would finish the task. The only thing left to do was to start exploring.

The lake just past the road proved to be the most inviting. We could see almost the entire lake from our site. It was a dark blue kidney-shaped lake with steep rock bluffs and rolling hills all around. It looked like the perfect size for a half-day adventure. Before we left Jim made a quick sketch of the lake in our logbook. I think he wanted to capture the moment without film. Just like explorers from the past.

It was a good five or six hours before we finished with our excursion. The camp did not change at all. Every item was just as we left it. Not like back home where items left out, were invitations to thieves. Even the keys to the jeep were still in the ignition. This was great, no worries, and besides Jim said "I didn't think we needed a spare set of keys."

We put everything away and ate a light dinner just before a quick storm rolled in. We could smell the rain coming in the freshening wind and hear big claps of thunder as it got closer. This proved to be the perfect time to hit the hay. Sleeping in a tent during a light thunderstorm can be a great experience, almost hypnotic in a way, with the clatter of thousands of drops hitting the nylon roof and the tent fabric snapping in the gusting winds. The only thing that woke us from a sound sleep was a trickle of water running through the tent. In just a few moments everything was readjusted, and we fell right back to sleep.

A few hours later John woke up and the tips of his ears were hurting from sunburn. Nowhere else was affected from the walk around the lake, just the tip of his ears. We suspected the army field cap he usually wore was the culprit. It made his ears stick out from his long hair. Tender ears that hadn't seen the sun in many, many years. It doesn't sound like much but they sure were burnt. It sucked for the rest of the night and the next few days. For a side sleeper, this is a big deal! So, when Jim went to town the next morning, aloe for sunburn was at the top of the list of things to get.

In the morning, as we climbed out of the tent, we could see all new tree branches and small sticks all about the campsite. It looked just like the day we arrived. We were starting to wonder if this storm was going to be a daily experience. We discovered that in the Black Hills there is a tree-shaking storm blowing thru almost every night.

A few campers visiting the outhouse stopped and let us know we could expect a quick shower every day just after dinner. We think they said it had something to do with the Black Hills. At least with storming almost every day, there should be no, what they call, widow-makers, (dead trees and or branches that could fall on us while we slept) messing with us in the middle of the night.

Jim wanted to pick up some well-deserved perishable items like fresh bread, eggs, and, of course, some aloe. John wanted to dig a small trench around the base of the tent. We thought this might prevent the water from running through the tent like the night before. The tent was now shaded, we just had to get rid of the water problem. John's interest in digging was because that the side he slept on was on the uphill side of the tent. It's not that it was a steep hill, it's just that water came right through the center of our camp before soaking into the ground. It is called surface run-off or sheet draining. Either way, if we stayed in the way, it's going to find us, the same as the night before.

When Jim arrived back from town, he said the little store he got the food at, was a dump. It had what we needed, but he wasn't looking forward to going back again. The town, Custer, although small, had some personality. This opened up an opportunity for some urban exploring on another day.

After we ate some of the fresh treats Jim picked up, we headed back to town. We walked down the street and stopped at the bench in front of the café protected from the sun by the covered planked sidewalk. Between the burgers cooking in the bar near the main intersection, we got a nostril full of diesel exhaust as the giant logging trucks roared by. Every day, starting at 10:00 AM. An old Native American woman would slowly ride by on her horse. She could have been sixty or she could have been a hundred years old. Either way, she had a weathered look to her. As interesting –looking, as she was, we did not want to be on her bad side. Native Americans can be a very vengeful group of people as we would learn later. She went by silently without any directions to the horse, and went directly to the senior center on the edge of the main street, tied up her horse, and went inside for several hours of bingo. When John told his mother about the horse, she told him of his great grandfather delivering milk by horse in the early years of Chicago. The horse, Dolly would walk the same route every day. At the end of the route, he would stop for a drink before heading home. The horse would take over and walk home without direction. When they got home the horse would just stop in her stall and eat what was set up for her before they left. After a few hours he would wake up and it was time for him to eat.

The following morning the sun shone bright, we were dry and rested, with no place to be. What could be a better way to start the weekend? Fresh eggs were on the breakfast menu with toast and coffee, that's how.

After a short nap, it was time for another hike. Our walk around the campground brought us to the main entrance. This is where we have to pay the two dollars each day we stayed at the national park.

The lake at the base of the campground that our campsite overlooked had large boulders on one side and a meadow on another. The rest of the lake had tall pines that came up to the banks. It reminded me of a picture out of a fishing magazine. It was too bad neither of us were into fishing. Although we did have some of the lures, hooks, bobbers, and twine in our survival kits. We thought it might be a good idea if we tried our hand at it just in case, we needed to use this skill in the great white north. We pulled out a small assortment of tackle from our survival kit and headed to the lake. We found a small sapling that was about ten feet long and set it up with ten to fifteen feet of line, hook, and a bobber. Jim turned over a rock and found a worm just the right size for the hook. With our lack of fishing skills or lack of fish in the lake, we did not catch anything in the one-hour attempt. Looks like it will be another night of beef stew.

Custer to Mount Rushmore

After we ate breakfast, we packed up for a day trip to Mount. Rushmore. We decided to take the top down and air things out a little since it was a beautiful day. With the PB&J sandwiches in one hand and the water in the other, we were off. The cameras were in the jeep so we would not forget them. John always made sure that he had the camera. We liked to travel light because it made packing and unpacking easier. We found out early on there was no need to take any more than we needed to for the day.

As we pulled out of camp, our adrenalin was pumping. It's not every day you can see one of the seven wonders of the USA. And who knows what we will find or do along the way. Once more we were "back on the road again," We had all the time in the world.

The main intersection in downtown Custer consisted of a three-way stop. The northern route would take us up to Mt. Rushmore. We expected about forty minutes or so to drive. After all, it was only twenty-five miles from our campsite. But we had the knack of going off the main road and going where we thought no man had gone before.

We were only on the road for a short time before the traffic started to back up. It appeared that the main route to Mt. Rushmore was under construction or everyone and their brother decided to go see it at the same time we did. It turned out to be construction. Traffic was at a complete stop for so long that we turned off the jeep just to let the engine cool down and save on gas. At one of these "stops," we saw a narrow path that looked like an old logging road heading up into the hills. Since we weren't going anywhere sitting in traffic, what the hell, off we went.

The jeep had incredible traction. It went up steep inclines and over large obstacles without hesitation. Maybe it had something to do with the non-directional tires, but the transmission and transfer case appeared to be right at home on the rough terrain. The short wheelbase caressed the path, just like the wind in a sail. Thanks to Jim's magnificent job rebuilding it during the school year, it performed flawlessly.

The path opened up into a small clearing surrounded by tall fragrant pines where the ground was covered with a carpet of long pine needles. Through some of the smaller trees, we could see that we were on the side of one of many rolling hills that overlooked a small meadow. The rocks or boulders that made up the hills rose about five hundred to a thousand feet with each lift in the roll. Most of the boulders were about the size of houses and some the size of cars. This looked like the perfect place to pull out a PB&J and take in the view. It sure beats looking at someone's bumper in the hot sun. So, we picked a rather large boulder about seven hundred feet above the meadow. As we were sitting there, we could see straight down to the basin below. If we were to fall, there would be no survivors. The only thing that met their death was our sandwiches. Those demolished, it was time to move on.

The traffic thinned out a little after lunchtime, so, we thought we better get going if we were going to make it before the monument closed up. After a few more turns in the road, there was a spot cleared off to the side so we could see the monument in the distance. We thought it looked like a good place to take some pictures. We even found a structure to climb, a lookout tower of sorts, to get a better look. After climbing to the top, it turned out to be a waste of time, after all, the view would have to be pretty spectacular to beat what we saw on top of our picnic boulder at the top of the logging path we'd just been at. The view turned out to be no better than what it looked like at the bottom of the tower, some fifty feet below.

The only thing that was memorable with the lookout tower was the fact that my camera fell out of my pocket and down about thirty feet to the ground. It looked kind of like slow motion. Bouncing off the timbers, and spinning as it fell onto a small rock, splitting in half at the end of its journey. Then the film popped out, as it hit the ground and a small dust cloud appeared. It looked pretty cool, but the camera was shot from that point on, and all the pictures taken in it was lost.

If we had been still stuck in traffic like the everyday tourists, we'd consider this humdrum stop a good leg stretcher, and a chance for the kids to get out of their parent's hair for a little while. It could have broken up a long drive. But we just got back on the main road from our excursion up the logging trail for thirty minutes. We decided to just two-track on logging roads for the rest of the way to Mount Rushmore.

When we finally pulled into the parking lot, we could see just the impressiveness of the stone sculpture of Mount Rushmore. From that distance it was flawless. We thought that the amount of detail given to each president did give the place a world-class rating. Jim remembered, just before the trip watching the movie *North by Northwest*, where they showed people walking around, and climbing on the heads. Somehow in the back of his mind, he thought maybe we could climb on the heads also.

It soon became apparent from all the signs along the walk, and stairs leading to the main building, they did not want anyone to wander off the main walks. There were fences and gates everywhere. The only way up probably would have been through the back way. Then we would still have to deal with the park rangers. And they looked like ex-Green Beret just looking for some reason to put their training in action and justify their existence. The last thing we wanted to do was to star in an action movie. So, we just went with the flow following the crowd, and headed to the main observation platform.

Once up there, John thought it was sort of a letdown, not because of the magnitude of the structure. There was a small museum with all the facts on the building process. And the pictures were nice, and some of the equipment was nice to touch. But it all seemed to leave out the one small element that we needed, climbing. After being cooped up in the Jeep all day, except for a little rock scrambling, we wanted some physical activity We arrived at Mount Rushmore about three o'clock, and had seen all we wanted to see and maybe more by somewhere around five. Maybe it wasn't so much the park, but the trip there that made the trip worthwhile. It took us five or six hours to get there, so we had no idea how long it would take to get back into town. We climbed into the Jeep ready to face the long haul back, and possibly have to eat in Custer.

When we rounded the corner in downtown Custer about forty-five minutes later, at 5:45 we got a good laugh. Traffic was light, it was still daylight, and we didn't run over any small animals on the road. Animals seemed to be a road hazard as the road was littered with carcasses, with roadkill every couple of miles.

It was a long time since our PB&J, and the last thing we wanted to do was to go back to camp, take an hour and a half to build a fire, cook dinner, take another half an hour to eat, and have to clean up in the dark. It somehow was against the camper's code of ethics to do anything in the dark, except to sit around the campfire. As seemed to happen frequently in the Black Hills, very dark clouds began to move in quickly, followed shortly soon after by a stiff wind and booming lightning and thunder. We both jumped up quickly without making a peep between us. After all our time together, it seemed we both knew what the other was thinking without the need to say anything out loud. One of us went to the driver's side and the other to the passenger side of the Jeep. We quickly pulled the top up over the roll bar in unison and slipped it into the channel on the windshield frame. We each grabbed our respective doors, slipped them into their mounting sockets and latched them shut just before the rain started to hit. Within the next few minutes, the raindrops started to fall. We set out to find food in town.

Our choices were simple, the town bar or the drug store fountain counter. We thought about it for a split second and said it's time for a beer. Although we began drinking in our early teens, in South Dakota we could do it legally. We were eighteen; legal age for beer and wine in several western states. We figured we earned a nice treat after the long day we just had. We walked through the door and the single room was not as dimly lit as some bars we had seen; we got a strong whiff of stale beer and musty air as we headed up to the bar.

As we perched ourselves on the barstools, it was like going back in time. Signs of olden times dwarfed any signs of present days. We joked about some of the bottles like no one touched the dusty bottles in over a hundred years and whether the company still existed. If those bottles could only talk, what stories they could tell? Who knows maybe someone will write a book about the stories bar bottles have someday?

On the wall opposite the bar was a large cartoonish mural depicting an old west gunfight with one cowboy lying on the floor bleeding. It was very colorful and simply done. We asked the bartender about it and she explained that it depicted a killing that happened in this bar during the last century. Who knows, maybe it was one of her relatives that were bartending and didn't like someone asking a lot of questions? There was one other thing that caught our eye, and that was buffalo burgers. We thought, perfectly western and how tasty. This was for us, burgers and beers. What a great way to top off the day.

The bartender was a heavy woman who looked like she had settled many fights with a swift backhand from her side of the bar. She was very pleasant to talk to if one-word sentences fulfilled your conversation needs. Then we saw a handgun, a black police-style-38 revolver sitting behind the bar, we jokingly said to each other "wonder what she needs that for." With that, she turned around and somehow knew what we said from fifteen feet away. The last thing we wanted to do was to get kicked out in the rain or worse, a picture on the wall of two guys on the floor bleeding. So, we shut up and sipped our Coors beer on tap, which was known in the Chicago area as "Rocky Mountain donkey p***". It tasted pretty good under the circumstances, so we ordered more. After a dozen or so beers and some mighty good buffalo burgers, it was time to head out.

The rain stopped a couple of hours before and magically dried on all the streets and walks. If you didn't see it or hear the thunder and see the rain coming down earlier you never would have known it rained at all.

The beer was a great treat, even though we drank a lot, we only had a mild buzz. We laughed all the way, back to the camp, and had no problem falling asleep that night.

A Few Weeks in Custer, South Dakota

Over the next few weeks, we spent a lot of time in downtown Custer. We became sort of honorary locals bestowed on us by nods of acceptance from the true residents we came in contact with so far. We enjoyed coming into town for a couple of hours at our regular scheduled time and sitting in a couple of old wooden chairs outside the general store. On quite a few occasions travelers heading to Mount Rushmore would ask us for directions. While we were there, we invested in a couple of really nice suede fringe jackets made by Jo-O-Kay in Oklahoma, and hats to match. Ironically, we never wore them in town.

One of our days heading to town we decided to stop at the major tourist attraction that we passed every day as we came to town: the crumbling remnants of Fort Custer. The ruins were a replica that was built as a tourist destination and then fell into disrepair. While walking around grass-covered paths, the remaining pieces of picket fence, and dilapidated ponderosa pine log cabins, we could still imagine how a fort in the area at the time of Custer and the 7th Cavalry may have been. A series of signs explained some of the features of the old fort and the geography around the town.

Across the main road to town from the ruins of the fort, sat an old house trailer in slightly better condition than the fort so after exploring the fort we decided to walk across the street and take a closer look. A white-haired character that had the appearance of a prospector, sat in a lawn chair in the shade under a canopy jetting out above the front door. He was heavily adorned with turquoise and silver jewelry. Randomly distributed around the front of the trailer were several rickety folding tables covered with a variety of rocks, petrified wood, and geo-crystal balls sliced in half, as well as a large variety of tumble-polished stones. The tabletops showed the ware and delimitation that comes from constant exposure to the weather as not being designed for outdoor use. We walked around the tables. Amazed at the size of some of the petrified wood pieces. When we felt we had seen all he had to offer we thanked him for letting us review his goods, and we headed on into another day in town, and then back to camp.

After several days in this camping spot, we awoke one morning to a new couple that had camped just across the road from us next to the lake. They were a young couple we guessed our age or maybe younger they seemed to have almost no gear, just a few blankets, and were having real trouble starting a fire. The guy called over "good morning" when we met glances. We had a full pot of coffee and he seemed friendly enough so Jim invited them over for a cup. The only rule when invited to someone's campfire for coffee, is to bring your coffee cup. The host will always have their spin on what they call coffee.

They gladly accepted, being very frustrated with their fire-making effort. After introducing themselves as Mark, and Becky, they asked if we had a kettle, they could borrow as they had forgotten to pick up utensils when they bought their food. We gladly accommodated them with one of our pots and some utensils, they promised to return as soon as they were done. They took the cooking equipment and a cup of coffee and went back to their camp. That night we invited them over for our campfire and some more coffee, they explained they were from

Lincoln, Nebraska, and they had decided to leave home because they wanted to get married and their parents were against it. They were traveling in Mark's red 66 Plymouth Sport Fury 440 muscle car that had the back end lifted, with matching Micky Thompson wheels and racing tires, that looked as though it was not too economical to operate and may give them some trouble. They were a nice couple and we wished them well when the evening ended, they went back to sleep in their car as they did not have a tent.

The next morning, as we were waking up, we heard the unmistakable roar of a diesel engine running at a high idle. We sprang from our bags, fully awakened by banging as if someone was pounding on an oil drum with a baseball bat.

Quickly surveying the area in the direction of the racket we could see a tank truck at the boat ramp. We got dressed and headed down the path to the launch. We arrived just in time to see the truck begin dumping thousands of small game fish into the lake. Several kids on their bicycles were there to see the spectacle.

Interestingly, it was here, at this location, at this time we stopped writing in the short-lived journal. Maybe we just became complacent in our new surroundings or did not feel the need to record the adventure for anyone else. Because from this point on every memory was for each of us to remember as we saw it or wanted to remember it.

So, you might say, the storytelling starts here.

Photo Journal

Rebuilding the Jeep (Torching off the plow.)

Jim and John Graduate High School

Jim and John loading the Jeep

Jim and John ready to leave Illinois

Somewhere in Iowa

Setting up before a storm in Iowa.

Jim in passenger seat, Sioux City Iowa.

First morning in Custer

Drying clothes after a storm in Custer

Short cut to Mt. Rushmore

John eating PB&J on the way to Mount Rushmore

Almost to Mount Rushmore

Rest after trip to Mount Rushmore

John claims his hand still hurts from hot spring in Yellowstone

On Lake Louise

The bunkhouse, British Columbia

The horses Jim and John rode

Haystack as big as a house that Jim and John stacked.

Waking up in Alberta, Canada

Jim in his new threads (Rifle from Montana, coat from Custer)

List of food

4 Cans Shoe string potatoes
2 Cans Spam
4 Cans Sliced Carrots
2~~8~~ Cans Sweet Corn
1~~8~~ Cans Corned Beef hash
3 Cans Sweet Peas
2 Cans Sliced Pineapple
4 ~~Cans~~ Tomato Paste.
~~5~~ Cans Beans **15**
~~2 Cans~~ Chilli
1~~8~~ Cans Beef Stew
1 Can Orange Segments
1 Can Tomatoes
~~1 Can Halves Bartlett Pears~~
1 Can Coffee
1 Can Shortening
1 Can Quaker Oats
1 bottle Syrup
1 Can Spinach
1 Container Salt
6 Packets Tang

MAURICE GEORGE D'AOUST
(Top Row 2nd From Right

Chateau Lake Louise
Canadian Rockies

Maurice worked as a Chef
19YRS OLd

Seein' Snakes?

ED BELLMORE'S ANNUAL
RATTLESNAKE HUNT SUN.

A brave and hardy group of hunters will take to Wheelingland wilds on Sunday, August 19, on Ed Bellmore's annual Rattlesnake Hunt.

The hunt is open to all adults. Starting point is at Bill's Place at 1:30 p.m.

Hunters are requested to wear knee-length boots, and be provided with a five-foot forked stick.

The search will fan out along the Forest Preserve north of Wheeling. Last year, conducted by the Northbrook Sports Club, the hunt bagged nine rattlers. The year before, three were snared.

The rattler in question is the Massauga Rattlesnake, a midwest cousin of the Diamondback. The Massauga is short and thick, and usually is under two feet in length, although slightly larger specimens have been found.

The Massauga Rattlesnake has a diet of mice, frogs, young rabbits and smaller snakes. They will also raid the eggs and young of ground-nesting birds.

Their bite is fatal, and they are usually found with the warning rattles, although it's not always sure if they sound their warning before striking. For example, hunters stepping on one will sometimes get bitten without warning.

Despite the dangerous aspects of the hunt, Ed Bellmore, mighty hunter, mighty fisherman, who conducts the annual safari, reports that he hasn't lost a customer yet.

The customary anti-snake venom may be obtained at Bill's Place in pints, fifths and shots.

Last Day in Custer, South Dakota

We spent the better part of two weeks in Custer and a total of seventeen days on the road. We did not listen to the news on the radio often and had no idea what the weather forecast was in the future, and we did not care. We did know that we had dumped a lot of the anxieties and concerns about open road travel. Explored all that Custer had to offer on the surface and behind the curtain, so to speak. We also made so many friends that we regret not writing their names down. But we do talk about them from time to time with a laugh or a what the hell was the matter with them. We did play music from Jim's extensive cassette tape collection. Well, for the few tapes we brought. So, the selection for this morning was Bachman Turner Overdrives "Roll on Down the Highway". It seemed appropriate for the situation. It was time to move on.

The sky was clear, the ground had dried from the nightly rain just after dinner time the night before and the temperature was in the low seventies! This along with the desire to get on the road made breaking down the camp fast and easy. Like everywhere we stayed, we left it in better condition than when we arrived. As a bonus, we left a supply of firewood for the next guest. It just seemed like the right thing to do.

As Jim started the Jeep and pulled on to the gravel road just in front of the campsite, he stopped, and we both took a last look at the spot we knew and could call our home for the past two weeks. We knew that we may never come back to this spot again, or be able to relive the experiences we had here. There was no need to write down our feelings. This spot, at this time, changed us forever.

Our last day in Custer was a lot like the first except we became a familiar sight. The wooden chairs in front of the general store sat empty like they were eagerly waiting for the next two travelers to take over. The old Native American woman we saw began to nod hello to us when she saw us. The day we left, instead of a nod, we gave her a short wave as a goodbye. She answered with her short wave as she knew we were on our way, like so many other travelers she must have seen in her many years.

We were leaving a place we both felt comfortable in and we both liked. It was so laid back; everyone just moved a little slower, took the time to say hello, how are you, and meant it. Because we were about 95 miles from the Pine Ridge Indian Reservation, a lot of the people we interacted with within the stores and just walking around town were originally from Pine Ridge. Back home, the Chicago area is known as a melting pot of diverse groups of people. Except for Native Americans. We did however have almost every forest preserve named after a local tribe from the past. But no Native American people to speak of.

We started to head north on 385 to the next town about 56 miles away. It took us around two hours to get to Deadwood, giving us enough time to listen to almost three cassette tapes. The hills and valleys were still just enough to block a radio signal.

As we got closer to town things started to be different. We didn't think we were away from a society that long. But some of the people in the cars that passed us were taking a long hard stare. Some were even pointing. Could it be the leather hats we bought in Custer? The long hair? Maybe they never saw a Jeep before? We never figured that one out.

There was no question that there were a lot of cars on the road. It was like a mass exodus from a disaster. When the town was in sight you could also see the presence of law enforcement. We are not talking about two squads parked side by side talking. No, cars were being pulled over everywhere by marked and unmarked cars. Since we could only do a little over thirty miles per hour, we knew we were not going to get pulled over for speeding so, we just kept going and drove past all of them until we got into Deadwood.

There were no more cars in front of us and no one walking on the streets. When we made a turn down a side street there were about six unmarked cars with people holding handguns standing behind their car doors for protection, looking in the direction we were heading. It looked like a low-budget TV show in progress. Some of the guys with guns started to yell at us as we passed their cars, what are you crazy? Are you trying to get yourself killed? And the one that stuck in our mind the most was the big guy yelling, "TAKE COVER."

What the hell happened while we were in Custer?

We were kind of committed to the direction we were heading and all the police cars made it impossible to turn around so, we just pushed the pedal to the metal and went through whatever was going on. No one chased us, no shots were fired all was good, right?

We pulled up in front of a small diner close to noon ready to treat ourselves to a nice cheeseburger and fries. The first thing the waitress said when she walked up to our table was, "How did we just drive through the shootout?" We just said we didn't want to get shot so we just sped up.

Well, that answer seemed to satisfy her so she took our order. When she came back with our coffee, she filled us in on what was going on in town. It's not that we asked. She just had a lot of free time. The diner was empty; we were her only customers and our burgers were sizzling on the grill.

Two FBI agents were looking for someone in connection with an outstanding federal warrant for robbery, the day before, she told us. As we were traveling through, there was a big shootout in Pine Ridge on the reservation.

The FBI agents spotted a red and white vehicle that this person was known to have. Little did the officers know, one of the three people in the vehicle had an outstanding warrant in Wisconsin for the attempted murder of an off-duty police officer. This guy was also traveling with members of the American Indian Movement. Who were also, like him, known to be armed and very dangerous!

It was around noon when the officers pulled them over. As they were calling in for backup a firefight opened up that lasted for about ten minutes. In those ten minutes, the FBI agents only managed to get off five rounds between them while the occupants along with other bystanders put more than one hundred and twenty-five rounds into their cars. The agents were wounded and then executed.

None of the men were who they were originally looking for were in the vehicle that was pulled over. The event that happened on June 26, 1975, is now known as "The Pine Ridge Shootout."

It was about then that the cook delivered our food because, like the waitress, he had little to do and wanted to add his spin. He said that the killers were still on the loose and they had word that they were heading up into Canada on 385 and probably getting on 85 after Spearfish. He told us that every single law enforcement officer wanted to be the one who caught the guys. That is why there are so many cars getting pulled over and everyone has an itchy trigger finger.

Now that was some useful information, we could have used twenty minutes ago. We looked at each other and said, note to ourselves, don't ignore police and drive through what might be an active crime scene. It was a good thing we were planning on going west on 14 to 90 and on to Yellowstone.

Needless to say, we now kept an eye out for anything that might be out of place. Well at least for a few hours. That was now in the past and we were driving into the future.

Just a note, the lead person of interest in the killing was captured by the RCMP in Alberta, Canada, in February of '76. More than likely, we were traveling on the road with them at some point!

After leaving Custer we continued west through Newcastle where the terrain changed from the wooded Black Hills to a more craggy and scarcely wooded terrain. A dry earthy smell replaced the sweet smell of the ponderosa pines.

As we pushed west, we came through the Absaroka Range and the Box Canyon where Chief Joseph in 1877 famously escaped the surrounding US Cavalry with his band of mostly women and children during his attempt to make it to Canada. When Chief Joseph surrendered that October to the pursuing soldiers to end his people's suffering, he said;

"Hear me, my chiefs! I am tired. My heart is sick and sad. From where the sun now stands, I will fight no more forever."

This was very inspiring to both of us. We could imagine his band working their way through what they believed to be impassable canyon trails in silence with cloth on the horse's feet so their pursuers did not know they were escaping in the night.

We continued through a beautiful and rugged country until we came to the arched stone gate of a National Forest in an arid and rocky area with rolling hills. We passed through and drove on the gravel road for an hour or so until we came to another stone archway that said Leaving the National Forest. We saw nothing in between except scrub grass and rocks.

We now had a three hundred and eighty-plus-mile drive across some of the most spectacular landscape Wyoming had to offer to get to our next destination, Yellowstone National Park. But, with all the sights, we pulled over at almost every opportunity! This of course just about doubled our drive time.

Yellowstone National Park, Wyoming

The morning of the July 2nd, after a solid night of driving the sun started to rise behind us. The shadow of the Jeep was long on the road in front of us when the sun hit the back window. The shadow seemed to get shorter as each minute passed. It's amazing how the sun can revive you after a somewhat uneventful drive. But, starting a new day in a new place is kind of exciting and gets the blood pumping. Sort of like the first snow of a new season.

For us growing up in the Midwest, we anticipate the first day of snow. There are many days of snow but there is only one first day. When that snowfall happens at night, and you open the living room curtains in the morning you see that fresh snow! Well, there is a burst of energy and excitement. It's probably different for everyone in different parts of the country but for us, it's that moment.

About that time reality started to set in and we took stock in our immediate surroundings. Not the outside, but the inside of the Jeep. It was trashed. Bad. All the food we ate was in wrappers or cans. Because we never threw trash out on the road, it had to go somewhere. And that somewhere was the floor of the Jeep. Most of the time we could just step on it and it would crush down to a flat almost nothing, but the cans took a little more effort. Mix that with four or five packs of cigarette butts that started in the ashtray but, always ended up bouncing out onto the floor. In hindsight we probably could have dumped the trash when we got gas but, that didn't happen too often and when it did, we were so focused on protecting the windshield and getting back on the road we didn't think to empty the trash.

Over the next hour or so we noticed more signs directing us to this place to eat, or that place to stay, and of course Yellowstone National Park. The excitement of the new experience was almost unbearable. The entrance of the park started to come into view. The huge timbers, the massive log-built building, and the mountains in the background lit up by that morning sun. We were there.

We arrived at the east entrance of Yellowstone National Park on July 2nd after crossing the Absaroka Range. It was just before the park opened at 8 am when we pulled into the drive-up lane at the massive entrance. The ranger sitting at the window waved at us and pointed to the clock and said that they open at eight. We waited ten minutes. What else could we do? There was no conversation, and we thought that was odd. He just kept looking at some papers and writing little notes in the sidebar. Maybe he was working out some sort of to-do list. Who knows? Then, without looking at the clock, he looked at us and said "welcome to Yellowstone National Park."

It took us twenty-four, non-stop hours driving on Federal Highway 14/16/20 to get there but, we made it. We were the first ones at the gate and paid the $7.00 entry fee that we thought was kind of steep for just a day pass, but it gave us what they called the "Golden Eagle" Pass (sticker for the windshield) and a map of the park that later would become invaluable.

As we drove in on the Sylvan Pass you could smell the pine trees and a slight sulfur smell. There was a slight breeze coming out of the west so we figured that the sulfur smell came from the hot springs. We were just amazed at the sunlight cutting through the towering pine trees and splashing the nearby peaks so proudly in the morning sun. Cody Peak at 10,267ft and Avalanche Peak at 10,566ft were the first mountains to welcome us before we went through the pass. Our amazement fizzled after we opened the map and found out that we had sixty-five miles to drive to get to Old Faithfull. More hours in the Jeep!

We pulled over at the first restroom sign we saw. It was very clean not like the campgrounds and gas stations we were used to using the past few weeks. It had running hot and cold water and flush toilets. What a treat to do a quick wash-up after the long drive. The one thing that unlike anything we had seen before was all the posters all over the walls and even in the stalls. They were all about bears and what to do and not to do: Do not feed the bears; Do not get out of the car to take pictures of the bears (like this would help us with soft side plastic doors); Do not run if you see a bear. The signs also advised us on what to do when attacked by a bear. Not if but, when! We were sure it was a misprint but it sure was an eye-opener. To steal a phrase from Dorothy in the Wizard of OZ she said to her dog Toto "We are not in Kanas anymore." Neither of us knew for sure if Kanas has bears but it sounded good. From that point on we knew that for the rest of the trip we could not let our guard down. That one-stop made us both resolved to try and keep the Jeep a little cleaner.

We drove a little less than twenty miles before we got to Lake Butte 8,348ft. This was about a mile to Yellowstone Lake so you could not get a real good view. Just to give you an idea of the height of some of the peaks around where we were, Yellowstone Lake is at 7733ft. That would make Lake Butte only 615ft higher. Kind of just a hill when you think about it. But we are in Yellowstone so most of what we are calling hills are over a mile above sea level.

We were making a pretty good time even though we wanted to stop everywhere. After a few more miles we were at Lake Village, at the northern end of the Lake and where the road crosses the Yellowstone River. by the way, Campers had to have hard-side campers or trailers in this area Our guess: probably because of the bears.

For the next twenty or so miles we drove south right along the lake with spectacular views until we got to West Thumb. Here we went west passing through Craig Pass, by Scaup Lake and Kepler Cascades before we arrived at Old Faithful.

We took three hours to drive, the 60 miles to Old Faithfull moseying along taking in all the scenery. Wouldn't you know, The Geyser erupted just before we got there.

Lucky for us there was a restaurant not far from Old Faithfull. The restaurant was a large lodge built-in 1904. It was the biggest log structure in the world. But it wasn't open. We asked the only person we saw what time they were going to open, and she said they were going to try for noon. It was eleven o'clock. She then started to tell us they closed for the past two days cleaning up because of the earthquake on the 30th. We must have had a shocked look on our faces because she said "you guys haven't heard about it? The Park rangers didn't tell you when you entered the park?" We said no we didn't hear anything because we just drove for twenty-four hours to get here and did not listen to any news on the radio. We never listened to the news, just music.

Jim asked if we could get a couple of cups of coffee while we waited for the restaurant to open and she said sure but we could not sit down. John thought she was the manager because she was not in a uniform. She did not want anyone to think they were open until the rest of the staff came in. We had no problem with that. As she walked up to us, the smell of freshly brewed coffee was overwhelming. It tasted so good and hot. Campfire coffee is always hot but, not always good. It has that unique flavor, campfire, with a hint of scorched coffee grounds. We thanked her and she picked up on our tone that it was a sincere thank you, not just polite thank you. She then stood by us and told us all about the earthquake.

It was 12:47 Monday, June 30th in the afternoon when a 6.1 magnitude earthquake hit the Norris Geyser Basin. To this date, it was the largest earthquake to hit within Yellowstone National Park. They say it was felt for two hundred miles around. The epicenter was only thirty miles north of Old Faithful within the Yellowstone Caldera part of the super-volcano in Yellowstone. As one park ranger said "there wasn't any noise at all. No dishes rattled and the ground just had a gentle roll." There were a few landslides and downed trees, and in a few areas some of the banks of the streams and rivers washed out. Oh, and Old Faithful is not so faithful anymore!

As of the day of the earthquake, the time can be off as much as thirty minutes or more. Park officials are still learning its new habits. The woman at the lodge advised us how to get a great seat: just wait until the next eruption and when all the people move on to their next stop you will have your pick. Sounds like a good plan, especially since we were late for the last eruption.

It was a little before noon and she told us our table was ready. We ordered cheeseburgers and fries and more coffee. After twenty-four hours of eating PB&J's and cold canned food, this was such a welcome treat.

We settled up the bill, thanked our waitress again, and went to find a front-row seat. After about five minutes we were almost asleep. We had to get up and walk around.

Not far away there was a path lined with a sagging rope attached to wooden posts every five feet or so. The hot springs were just past the ropes. Half-asleep, John stepped over the rope and put his hand into one of the hot springs as we walked down the path. Like Jim said the path was roped off to protect the tourists from doing just that and there were signs but, how hot could it be? Although he was almost comatose from the lack of sleep, he nearly fell over pulling his hand back at lightning speed. With surprise turning to agony on his face he said in a wide-awake voice, "that is hot!" About that time, we heard a faint whistle sound and thought this might be the start of Old Faithful doing its thing.

Sure, enough it was the start, and it was not disappointing. We were less than one hundred feet away when it went off. It was like a huge waterfall going in the wrong direction powered by a rocket engine. Glad we were upwind. It looked like it shot at least a hundred feet into the air a few times with quite a few smaller spurts. It lasted less than five minutes, but it sure still packs a punch. It was only a short experience for such a long journey but, it's not always about the event, sometimes it's the road to get there that puts the whole package together.

After it was over, it was time for us to get back on the road. As we walked through the parking lot, we overheard some people talking about the closed road sixteen miles north between Madison Jct. and Norris Jct. A closed road? That can't be good. We soon found out some very large boulders blocked the road in a few locations.

Out came our $7.00 map and low and behold that was our route to the north entrance at Gardiner, just north of Mammoth Hot Springs. If we did not overhear those people talking, it would have cost us over two hours of lost time backtracking. Well, we still had to backtrack a little, just to get on the new route. We now had ninety-six miles to go just to get out of Yellowstone. We figured, in ideal conditions, we could do it in five to six hours. We now had the aftermath of the earthquake to deal with.

As we made our way north and got closer to the earthquake's epicenter, we ran into a lot of construction traffic going to repair the blocked roads, fallen trees, and clear streams that were dammed up. They had their hands full for the next few weeks. We drove through a few washed out and flooded roads and at one point one lane was completely washed out. By the time we left the park, it was close to eight o'clock at night, twelve hours after we entered the park.

Singing Creedance – "Up around the bend", we crossed over into Montana with nowhere to camp. It will be another two days before we sleep.

The Drive Around Glacier National Park, Montana

We pushed hard after our stop in Yellowstone and we were nearly delirious after the sixteen, five-hundred-and-eighty-mile drive, having not slept in four nights other than a cat nap on the passenger side.

The Trip Tik promised that when we got into "Browning," we'd be near the entrance to Glacier National Park. That's when we knew we had some 75 miles to go until we got to a campground that suited our budget.

As we came closer to what we expected to be the entrance to the park we saw a rather ominous-looking barricade. We pulled into the general store across the street. Once inside a tall, lanky, and jovial fellow greeted us. He tooted upon seeing us, "What can I do for ya." We asked about the barricade. He proceeded to tell us about the 40 feet of snow blocking the road through Glacier and the sudden warming spell that is causing the rapid melt of that snow, thereby causing widespread flooding, washing out the only other road west for 150 miles.

After our jaws dropped, it must have been obvious that we were in a state of shock because the fellow changed his tone to one of dread. He said there was only one way through: around Glacier with a Jeep because the roads were virtually gone.

We instantly perked up and informed him that we were driving a Jeep, and thanked him for all the information. We spent a few minutes looking around the store for any supplies we could use and for any new cassette tapes, we may want to add to the Jeep's limited library of music. They had nothing in stock from the current decade and what they did have focused entirely on country and western genre.

We hopped in the Jeep with renewed energy in the anticipation of a new adventure. We headed south toward the other set of barricades on the road around Glacier. We slowly weaved our way through the barricades and on up the road. About a half-mile up the road, we encountered a roadblock manned by State Troopers We explained our goal of getting to the other side of Glacier before finding a place to spend the night. The Trooper's told us about the poor condition of the road and the road crew, that we saw just ahead working on a washed-out lane.

Officer Clancy warned us that if we get stuck out there, the crew could take three weeks to get to us. We expressed our intention to go on anyway.

The Troopers then proceeded to take a thorough inventory of our supplies. Do you have food for two weeks? Check Do, you have at least one good spare tire? Check. Do, you have extra fuel? "Check. They allowed us to proceed at our own risk, warning us to be careful especially where the bridges are gone.

As we passed the road crew working hard to restore the road, we felt a sense of excitement and adventure going where we would be truly self-reliant. We slowly left the crews behind us and proceeded to increase speed, as the area the crew was working on seemed to be the worst of it.

We began to wonder what all the fuss was about; it was beautiful countryside. The road wound along the side of the mountains following a gorge cut by a river we could see occasionally raging 3000 feet below us. On the opposite side of the gorge, about 3 to 5 miles we could see a railroad. The rail track was built on the sheer face of the mountain as the road we were on. Much of the track was covered with a tin shed-like roof to keep the tracks clear of snow and falling debris from the mountain. We no sooner realized this than we began to see patches of mud and rock sitting in the middle of the road ahead of us. Jim looked down at the river and began to notice large twisted steel structures in the water. After trying to figure out what they were for some time it hit us that they were pieces of bridges that had evidently been washed out and carried downstream by the raging current.

We were moving along at a pretty good pace, following the road as it wound its way along a sheer wall. The cliff face went straight up 1000 feet and down 3000 feet to the boiling river below. We came around the curve fast and to our horror, the lane in which we were traveling was completely gone, John jerked the wheel to the left and hugged the cliff face. He asked the white-knuckled Jim if he was okay. On the passenger's side, Jim saw gravel and bits of blacktop braking away under the front tire and rolling down toward the river, through the large crack between the canvas door and the side of the Jeep. "Just keep going," was all he said.

Jim remembers thinking that Officer Clancy was wrong, the road crews would never find us if something happened out here. To our dismay, this was just the first of several obstacles encountered on the path around Glacier. From that point on we really couldn't call it a road. We forded fast-moving streams, pushed fallen logs and boulders from our path, and at times wondered if we were still on the road. After 75 miles and 12 hours of gritting teeth and just holding on for dear life, we emerged a little older and a little wiser.

We passed the crews working on the roads from the west side of Glacier, they looked up at us from their work surprised that someone emerged from the road they were repairing. Happy at our victory at surviving our ordeal we shoved the *Creedence Clearwater Revival* tape in the tape player and cranked up "Up Around the Bend." We knew we would soon get a good night's sleep, something we hadn't had in four and a half days.

Eureka, Montana

We ate breakfast in Eureka one brisk early morning. This was one of the most typical types of diners in almost any town that was built in the fifties. We called them "strip centers" due to four or five businesses lumped together with the building parallel with the road all under one roof. All set up the same from outside appearances. What set them apart was their unique signs mounted on the building or mounted perpendicular to the street by steel supports and chains. The latter was the case here. The large windows in the front of the diner were without any posters or painted signage that a sign painter would do from time to time. The other establishments however seemed to want to hide anything that they were doing inside with almost all their glass-covered.

We walked in and sat down at the counter that was in a "U" shape with the seats looking out that window. This had a good view of the street and the hardware store across the street. It was nice to just sit there and watch the people just starting their day, going to work or whatever brought them out for the new day.

We were kind of surprised how many people were out and about. The menu was on the chalkboard above the kitchen pass-through window. The smell of bacon and hash browns permeated the room.

Without warning, Somone slammed a rifle down on the counter. Okay, maybe not a slam but, because it was kind of quiet, and it was not something we were used to, it sure seemed like a slam to us. Oddly no one else seemed to care?

We slowly began to scan the room with our eyes. We noticed everyone, except for the waitress, had a rifle or sidearm of some sort. We thought maybe the waitress concealed her firearm. Besides she didn't need one because she looked like she could take everyone out with her bare hands before anyone had a chance to put enough rounds in her to slow her down.

The odd thing was it wasn't hunting season. The scary thing was no one from home knew where we were. We got the feeling that we may never be heard from again if we said or did something they did not like. We kept our heads down and enjoyed the Number One special: bacon and eggs. The coffee was even better.

While we were sitting there, looking out the window we read some of the advertisements plastered all over the hardware store windows across the street. Most items were things we saw back home but, there was one that caught our eye: "Winchester." This was the rifle that changed the west. This was part of history. Like a moth to a fire, we had to go over and explore.

Jim had always wanted a long gun, especially a Winchester. It went with the fringe coats we bought in Custer so, why not take a look. We had the money. We finished a great breakfast, paid our check, and tried to walk calmly across the street while our legs wanted to sprint over there.

At first, it was like a normal, for us, classic hardware store. The checkout was right there as we walked in the door. A few aisles of popular items that people might be tempted to shoplift within sight of the cashier and then there it was, along the back wall, the firearms center. In an open box on display, leaning against the wall at the top of a display shelf above the back counter and almost touching the high tin ceiling, the soon to be purchased, Winchester.

Jim asked the clerk to take a look at it, and he got a ladder to get it down. Jim held it carefully in his hands and felt like he was a kid holding his first BB gun, but this was a beautiful 30/30 model 94. He told the clerk "I will take it." The clerk asked for Jim's Montana driver's license, which was an obvious problem.

The clerk hesitated for just a moment and looked side to side to see if anyone was looking. Leaning in close, he told us to go find a local to buy it for us. Locals can sell to anybody. Jim asked him to hold it for him and we went outside to find someone that would be willing to help.

The first guy we ran into seemed about our age only weathered as he worked outside on a ranch or farm. Walking right toward us, probably because we were standing in the doorway. We said the customary "morning," and he returned with the same. After our time in Custer, we got pretty familiar with how this greeting with the locals went. Customary greeting meant you are now acquaintances and are allowed to ask one question. If the reply is a one-word answer, they don't want to or, don't have time to talk. If they stop walking, make eye contact with you, and pause for just a second you could have a new friend. If the answer is more than two sentences, be prepared for what could be a very long answer to your question, and you are about to become friends. It doesn't take much and it happens that fast. A new friend will be willing to do any type of favor they are asked.

The question we asked was do you live in Montana?

Kind of an odd question but, it didn't seem to faze the guy in the least. "Yes, I do, lived here all my life, just outside of town."

Jim introducing us, and asking his name, "Jerry" he exclaimed, then testing our new friendship explaining that we are not from around here followed by the important question. Would you buy a rifle for us if we gave you the money? He said no because he wasn't old enough, but his brother Lenny is, and if you want, we can go get him? We agreed and headed out to get him. He is at a party not far from here, no less. Hard to believe, the first person we met when we walked out of the hardware store took us to a party. We imagined the store clerk looking out the window at us, grinning from ear to ear knowing he just made a sale.

Our new friend Jerry, extinguished his plans for shopping and moved on to something much more fun. He jumped into his late sixties Ford Ranchero and told us to follow him. We jumped in the Jeep and headed close behind up a steep incline overlooking the edge of town.

We stopped at what looked like a long driveway and our new friend said we had to come in on the backside of a brick ranch house because there was a big party going on and there would be nowhere to park in front. Jerry left his car and climbed into the back of the Jeep, as we had the rear soft plastic window rolled up, and tied. As we approached the house, we heard a massive burst of gunfire, not automatic but coming from several guns at the front of the house.

As we rolled up behind the house, we could see people bolting out of the back door, and running in all directions laughing. Our new friend yelled at a group of people just coming out the back door of the house, Lenny! And the yell caught the attention of a guy who turned out to be the brother of our new friend Jerry. He changed direction mid-stride and ran up to us and dove into the open back of the Jeep and yelled go, go, go.

Once he stopped laughing, he explained that the sheriff, the only law enforcement officer for 200 square miles, had attempted to break up the party and while he was at the front door all the guys at the party took a quick shot at his squad car through the windows. As we sped around the edge of the house, we saw the bullet-riddled squad car and the sheriff trying to catch any of the party-goers now running in all directions laughing hysterically. We now have two friends and one of them now owed us a favor. We stopped long enough to let Jerry get his Ranchero before we all headed back into town.

We returned to the Hardware store with our new friends and Lenny quickly purchased the Winchester and handed it to Jim as if nothing had happened. As Jim was holding his new gun, then Lenny reached into his pocket and handed him a box of 30/30 rounds and said "it's no good without these." What a guy.

We kept looking around anticipating flashing lights from the sheriff when the older brother Lenny said we should lay low for a while and asked us over to their house to kick back and party till the dust settled. Back home when we say kickback that means put some tunes on and party means to light one up and crack open a beer. How could we say no? When we saw the huge stereo and they started with the band Deep Purple's, *Machine Head*, we knew we were in no hurry to leave. Everyone in Eureka seemed to party hard on the weekend because they had a half barrel of beer on hand. Who knows what kind of beer it was but, it was cold. When the pizzas came, we threw a handful of money in the hat to pitch in our share. This was just like being at home except they asked a lot of questions about Chicago. It didn't matter that we were from a northern suburb. It was close enough for them.

Just about the time, we finished the pizza the house started to fill up with their friends. They were talking about the ruckus just outside of town and how the sheriff's car was shot up, again. We said it sounds like a dangerous job and they said not really, everyone is a really good shot and would never think about shooting the sheriff but, his car was another story.

It must have been well after midnight when we told them that we better get going and they said we might as well just crash there because the sheriff was going to pull anyone over that is out on the road at this hour. Hard to argue with that. We found a room downstairs and passed out.

In the morning the older brother was up and looking out the window and said you would have gotten pulled over for sure in a yellow jeep. He then told us to be careful because the Indians are all on edge lately especially near the reservations. He said it was funny last night but he now thinks there were a few Indians at the Ranch house the day before and that they were the ones that started shooting.

We thanked him for his help and got back on the road.

Trego, Montana

We took a detour from the planned trip prepared for us by The Chicago Motor Club to go into Trego, Montana. We had to double back from Eureka, as we had passed the road, we needed the day before. John's girlfriend, Debbie, traveled to Trego with two of her friends. They were off visiting family that lived deep off the grid. The girls planned to be there for some time. We hoped to stop by and see them as we would be in the general area but had no set date. It's a good thing because we had no clue where we would be or when, and there was no way to contact them, as they had no phone that we knew of and we had no address, other than Trego, but we were told it was a small town and we thought how hard can it be?

Trego had less than 100 people, so we figured we could find them. We pulled into Trego late one evening, about two hours before sunset, and looked for the largest tar paper shack in the downtown area. We left the Jeep on the dirt road and walked up a path thinking it must lead to the mayor's house or someone we could trust for directions. We figured everybody knew who everyone was.

We knocked stoutly on the skeletal remains of what once was a screen door, and we waited, for a rather long time considering the size of the shack, before two faces appeared in the door. The taller of the two looked to be a teenage boy and the shorter may have been his younger sister. It was kind of hard to tell. These two looked as though they had spent a great deal of time underground, they were covered in soot and what smelled like some type of manure. They both had this strange look of astonishment like they never saw people before. We asked if they knew where the Real McCoy's lived and they didn't say anything, so we thanked them for their considerable assistance, and returned to the Jeep. We continued up the largest of the two-track logging roads leading through town.

After what seemed like an eternity, we came to two small cabins. The sun about to set and we thought we better find a place to spend the night. We decided to ask at the cabins if we could camp in the nearby clearing. To our surprise, our search ended with our knock on the door. As the heavy rough sawed pine door swung open, we were met huge smiles from Debbie and her two friends Linda and Judy. They were so happy we could find the place with the limited directions they gave us. They said they did not know there was a shared phone we could have called them on. More than likely the residents did not tell anyone about it so no one would call them.

Debbie's friend Judy was somehow related to Bill and Lucy who were the owners of the cabin the girls were staying at. Lucy invited Judy and she asked if she could bring two friends to come and visit her and Bill in Montana. Lucy's husband, besides being a mountain man trapping and hunting, was a lumberjack cutting railroad ties when he needed money for supplies. After the introductions and the how-was-your-trip pleasantries, our need to crash became obvious, or so it seemed to us.

We asked if we could set up our tent in a small clearing on the other side of the road opposite the cabins, but they insisted we spend the night in the cabin. It did not dawn on us at the time but, this was grizzly bear country and with the smell of food on our tent, we would have possibly been a late-night snack for one of them. We pulled out the bare necessities and we spread our sleeping bags on the floor in the main room of the cabin and fell asleep in no time.

The two cabins were nearly identical, the one on the left from the road was where the girls were staying. The other cabin's main room was to be our campsite and Luther and his wife Marry were our hosts. The cabins were very modest, two rooms, the main or front room had the kitchen in the front right corner and the rest was the living room. It was about 14' by 12' in size. The rear of the cabin was the bedroom about 10' by 14'. Each cabin had three doors in a line from the main room to the bedroom and out the bedroom to the woods and a creek running past. The cabins were at least 100 years old, and one needed a roof which was made of tree slabs hollowed out and laid from peek to wall alternated bark side up and down in turn and overlapped to create a surface that would shed rain.

In the main room of each cabin was a copper kettle type, wood stove, based on a potbellied stove but much larger and made from copper-colored sheet metal. The stoves gave off a lot of heat and would burn hot all night without refueling. This was done by stoking the stove with a large log and adjusting the damper on the stove pipe along with the air intake on the front just before turning in. It was a real art to make sure you still had some embers to work with, in the morning. We had to be careful; the stove got very hot and we did not want to set up our gear so close that our bags could get damaged.

During the grand tour, we noticed the owner of the cabin had a Ruger Blackhawk .44 caliber pistol in the holster hanging on the bedpost. Just like in the old west including all the bullets in the belt. After some of the restaurants we visited, it did not shock us as much as you would think and we just thought it was backwoods law and order. John was very interested in the .44, so Luther our host pulled it out of the holster and showed it to us. There was no way he was going to let someone he just met touch one of his guns. It was sort of a dance that we both understood. He then pulled out a case that contained a customized bolt action Remmington XP100 pistol with a scope and custom-fitted barrel and double trigger. He explained how years before he had been a competitive marksman and had won many national competitions before coming to the Montana mountains.

One of the girls had to go to the outhouse before we all turned in, which was across the road. Luther, thought it would be a good idea to shoot off a round and spook her. So, he pulled out the Ruger with what he affectionately referred to as a rhino load (he loaded his own rounds) and snuck up to within three or four feet of the outhouse before squeezing off 4 rounds in rapid succession in the air. John said he was not looking forward to the next time he had to go. These guys were obviously not dealing with a full deck or to put it another way, they seemed a few bricks short of a full load.

We still don't know how we lasted the entire week without going to the outhouse.

In the morning, with a good night's sleep, we got a better look at our new surroundings. We saw that they had run power to the cabins from the power lines running along the logging road. A pay telephone hung on the pole between the cabins. We thought it was strange and we never saw this anywhere else but it did make sense. Neither of them had to pay a monthly phone bill and they could make a free call if there were any emergencies. If a call came in, the first person from either cabin would answer, the ringer was loud enough you could hear it inside. In the light of day, we saw that the infamous outhouse across the road, just past the ditch that ran along the road. Anyone taking a trip to the outhouse had to watch his step across a makeshift bridge crossing the ditch. The running water we thought was in the kitchen was actually behind the cabins from the rapidly flowing creek.

The McCoy's and some of their friends set up a hunt for elk days before we got there because they ran low on supplies. Nothing wrong with that, except, it was not in season for elk. That meant it is illegal, in other words, poaching. This was not sport hunting for them, this was survival. These guys have been working as a team for a long time and had a system.

One of the neighbors Dave, who we had not yet met, was the first to bag an Elk and he dragged it out of the bush and into the back of his Chevy Suburban that doubled as a makeshift butcher shop. It looked like they may have done this before. In less than 20 minutes that elk was parted and neatly stacked, the better cuts grilling while they worked. The wives were busy prepping the skins to be used as new coats and hats at a later date.

The next day a DNR Agent showed up looking very suspiciously at the bed of Daves truck. We suspected he knew what happened but did not have a trace of evidence. Just maybe, he was not looking hard. All the meat was divided up between the neighbors and anyone else who needed it. The evidence was nowhere to be found. According to the hunters, the state prison was not a good place to be. Four years at "Deer Lodge," as they called it was a long time to be put away, this was the average time for poaching if you were convicted. If you got arrested and you didn't have bail money, you had to sit in jail waiting for trial. We were lucky to be with the clever ones.

It did not matter if the Elk was poached, the steaks were deliciously grilled. We gorged ourselves on elk for the next week and, who could forget our introduction to the notorious rocky mountain oysters? The mountain boys didn't tell us what they were until it was too late to turn back. They laughed their asses off at us slack-jawed when we realized we had a craw full of elk testicles.

The morning after the big hunt we were treated to steak and eggs but with a twist. The steak was elk heart and only given to guests or the head of the household. With our acknowledgment that this was the best steak we ever had, we had now moved up the status level from stranger to the guest. The next step would be guest to a friend and with that status, our new friends showed us and let us handle their guns. In the north woods, this is one of the highest honors they could bestow on someone.

Jim woke up one morning looking up the barrel of a .44 caliber revolver. As his eyes slowly adjusted, he looked past the barrel at the gnarly-haired, toothless face of Dave, the guy who butchered the elk in the back of his pickup truck. Why he happened to be cleaning his gun in the chair just above Jim's head who knows. He began to laugh at Jim's widening eyes just below his pistol. Remember this is deep off the grid with little law out here and questionable sanity for some. So, any reaction could set off a chain of events with an unsavory outcome. Running through Jim's mind as he cleared the sleep from his brain, who is this guy and how long has he been watching us sleep? Dave, the grizzly man turned out to be a family friend and lived about ten miles further up the logging road.

One clear morning we decided to take the girls for a ride in the jeep, so we unloaded the remainder of our gear and pulled the top down. We all five of us jumped in and took a fun and bouncy drive up the old logging road. The bench seat in the back sure came in handy. We were all laughing and having a great time. We came to a logged clearing and noticed a plateau about 200 feet up a steep hill alongside the road and thought we would get a great view from up there. Rather than climb up, Jim thought it would be fun to see how the jeep would do climbing it. He backed across the road to get a running start and with locking wheel hubs and four-wheel-drive lever set into position, we started up the hill. We were moving pretty well when the Jeep jolted to a hard stop just before the top, it turns out we hit a tree trunk with the axle and we were forced to back down the hill riding the brakes all the way. Luckily the stump just put a dent in the differential cover and did not break anything. So, it was up the trail again but this time looking a little closer for those stumps that were hidden under all the brush.

No one was disappointed in the view and everyone thought this would be a great spot overlooking all the roads and the two-track paths the logging company had cut for the harvesting of wood. But of course, this was a business for them and this spot was probably going to be replanted with trees.

As we had been there sharing their hospitality and elk, we wanted to help them in some way to pay them back. We overheard the owners talking about the boards needed for the roof. The trees they had cut were now ready to mill and cut to size, but they could not use the sawmill during the week due to the production schedule. They could use it on the weekend, but they needed a few more people to run the equipment. We realized the roof needed work as the hollowed half logs that alternately overlapped to shed rain had become very rotten in many places, we thought we could help with this.

When we asked Bill and Luther if we could help, we felt their anxiety fade away and they both said, at the same time "hell Yeah." They ran out the door and jumped in their truck to round up the rest of the help needed for the next day.

We all met outside the cabin early in the morning after a big breakfast of elk and eggs. Two more of their friends pulled up in their pickup truck right on time. Kind of weird considering no one was wearing a watch and we sure didn't remember seeing a clock anywhere at the cabins.

We all loaded into their friend's truck and off we went to the sawmill. This was not a lumber yard; it was a sawmill. They took trees that were cut, stacked to dry, and then cut into boards to order. Piles of trees stacked up all around the building in almost a complete circle.

While we were taking it all in one of the guys said, as he was pointing, this is our stack. They said that if you worked for the mill, you could dry and cut your timber for free. Sounded like a great benefit for them. The owners of the mill probably figured the employees were going to do it anyway so might as well let them feel like they are getting a benefit.

One guy jumped in a front-end loader with an attachment on the front to pick up and move huge cut trees. Another started up and adjusted the mill to start the initial cutting of the raw timber. Another guy started the rough timber mill. Our job was going to be grabbing the fresh-cut boards and carry them out to the truck and load them in the back. To see these guys in action was just like watching them process an elk.

While we were humping the boards to the truck, we could hear someone shooting, one shot every so often. Not that you could time it. It kind of just caught us off guard. And it seemed kind of close. The shots came so quickly that we knew it was not someone hunting. Besides, the DNR would be there in no time because the sound echoed through the mountains.

When we took a break, we asked what all the shooting was, and should we be concerned? They all had a good laugh and said only if you don't pay him. They then proceeded to tell us that John Paul Homes was a sniper in Vietnam and was out on his own for so long that he now had trouble dealing with other people. He will talk to people if he has to, but he doesn't like it and he will let you know. All the homeowners and businesses around the mountain hire him to shoot the groundhogs to cut down on all the holes they dig. A person or an animal stepping in a groundhog hole will more than likely result in a broken leg and have to be put down. We weren't sure if he was just talking about animals. We are not sure which one of us asked if he ever misses? And the guys said, "you don't hear a second shot do ya?" Interesting, we asked how far away he was. One of the guys said two to three thousand feet, maybe more, once and a while. That is a half mile or more away!

The only time John Paul came down the mountain was to collect on his kills. He just reported how many he shot and the amount due. He also expected payment right away, mostly on the spot but would stop back in a few hours if he has to. We asked if anyone questioned his kills and they said no way, are you nuts? Did he ever have someone refuse to pay? They looked at each other and said there was a new guy who gave him a hard time about the kill count once. John Paul was not one to get into a debate. So, he just walked away, and the new guy thought he had the upper hand; Until the new guy was showing a neighbor how he had no groundhog holes on his property and going on about how he doubted if the kill counts John Paul gave him were accurate. Well, the neighbor was a little taken back because no one questioned John Paul's counts before. Besides. the price is so small it barely covered the cost of the bullet and he took care of the problem.

The newcomer pointed to a spot on his property as a small piece of wood, about three feet from his foot shattered followed by the sound of a gunshot three or four seconds later. John Paul was watching them through his rifle scope and figured a lesson needed to be learned. The newcomer told the neighbor that John Paul tried to kill him and he was going to call the authorities. The neighbor said that if he wanted to, John Paul would have just shot off your big toe, he was that much of a sharpshooter. From that point on no one offered up a question or problem.

Well, back to the lumber mill. It did not take long to cut enough wood to reroof the entire cabin plus a few extra. The truck was loaded well beyond its limits so it was a good thing we did not have far to drive. We got to the cabins a little after noon and had a quick lunch that the girls had prepared. The guys were talking about the plan of attack when they realized they did not have enough tools. Jim said no problem and pulled out hammers and crowbars. Their enthusiasm escalated as we began ripping off the old roof, with the new roof going up almost just as fast. By dinner time the roof was completed, and everyone stood around and complimented each other on a job well done. Needless to say, there was no problem falling asleep that night.

The next morning, Jim was telling Luther our host that he just bought a Winchester in Eurika and Luther offered to set the sites. He was an accomplished marksman and had won several competitions in his past. He checked the grain of the cartridges Jim had and at 150, he determined the expected arch, he then set up a small target at 25 yards, as he explained it, this would put the bullet in the same arch position at 150 yards. Luther took several shots at the close target and adjusted the site between each. When he felt satisfied, he had Jim place a dime at the 25-yard target, he was able to hit the dime dead center. He had Jim take a dime out to 150 yards as he had measured it. He then shot and hit the dime and handed Jim the Winchester and said he was happy with its accuracy and site adjustment. He told Jim to pay attention to the distances and if it was closer than 25 yards aim high and further than 25, but less than 150 aim low.

Later that morning the guys decided they needed to go for a bear hunt to start building up supplies for winter and this time they had a permit tag that they were not going to let go to waste. But we could not find John anywhere. Jim grabbed Bill and Luther and the three of them jumped in the Jeep and we drove up and down the road and around the cabin site into the woods across the road through some nearby clearings but no John, and incidentally, Debbie was missing as well. The guys were calling our hunt for John, bare-butt hunting.

An hour or so after Debbie and John "wandered off" they walked up to the cabin and everyone was sitting outside by the side of the cabin. At first, they were relieved that everything was ok. Remember, this is bear country and they did not have a firearm with them for protection. Then they started laughing because they knew what they were doing. They just didn't know where. These guys touted that they were such good trackers that they could track anything that walked. Well, that didn't work out so good for the mountain men in this case. At the same time, they were also impressed that John and Debbie did not leave a trail that they could track. But Bill and Luther would not let up until the couple told them where they were. The guys just wanted to go there and backtrack to find out how they missed our tracks.

After that, the guys said let's go get us a bear! We asked if we <u>all</u> needed to get a license? They had planned on whoever got it would get the tag they had as they were not doing this for fun or sport but, for food. We began our bear hunt by driving up one of the logging roads that our hosts knew well. After about two miles we parked the jeep.

The guys first pulled their backup pistols from their quick-draw holsters and made sure they were fully loaded with six cartridges. Not five like they had to do with older pistols or commonly called a cowboy load. Those would sometimes discharge if the hammer was hit or the firearm dropped. The newer ones had a safety device in the hammer assembly that would prevent that from happening. The next step that we noticed was something we didn't think about but, this was not their first time on a <u>bear</u> hunt. They holstered their pistols and did not slip the little loop over the trigger. That little piece of safety gear is to prevent the gun from slipping out of the holster if you fell or were running or even if you were on horseback. This step was not forgotten, and when they noticed us looking, and just about to remind them they said "you never know when a bear is going to charge you on a trail. "We kind of felt a little vulnerable from that point on. The guys helped ease our nervousness said they would put us in the middle of the line. Next, out came their rifles, they had a Winchester model 700 Alaskan that had a stainless finish and a Marlin 1895 lever action that was worn, but well taken care of. These were for the big game, brown bear and moose. Jim pulled out his new 30/30 Winchester 94 and John pulled out his 303 British Lee-Enfield No 5 MK 1. Luther asked if he could see it and John was happy to show him. He looked it over and knew it was a military rifle and it had seen battle but it was in great shape for its age. It had a short barrel and a flash-hider on it and a bayonet mount because it was, after all a military weapon. Luther's eyes got like saucers when removed the clip to see what kind of load John was going to use. Only someone who was in the military would notice the black tips, John had a full clip of armor-piercing bullets. He said he sure was glad he saw this because if a bear was shot with one or ten of these they would just go right through the bear and not drop him. The bear would continue to charge and be pissed off. Now if we needed to shoot one hiding behind a tree, they might need it. But for now, they said John should just be ready but not take a primary shot. Ok, good to know. All packed up and loaded, we all proceeded on foot.

After a few more miles we found signs of a great deal of bear activity on the narrow two-track road. In other words, bear poop and every couple of feet. John couldn't help thinking that it was odd that these bears will only shit on the road, The guys kept grabbing the "sign" in their hands to see how fresh it was, and if it was warm. We eventually came to a large clearing and we spotted a bear about half a mile up the side of the hill. We thought it was too far away to shoot, but these guys were marksmen. They knew if we hit it, we could be chasing it for days.

During our stay, we met several of Bill's and Luther's friends, each with a unique story of how they came to this place and the mountain-man lifestyle. One of their friends, Wyatt had to be coaxed in from the woods as he was shy from his years of isolation. The unfamiliar Jeep made him curious and eventually brought him closer and closer until the guys knew he was just past the trees and persuaded him to come and meet their guests.

Wyatt eventually warmed up to our presence and told us how he had grown up in the mountains of Colorado and walked through the mountains north until he found better hunting in Montana. He built a cabin near the tree line. He also told us how he met our Bill and Luther. After several years in Montana, he got word that his parents were coming to visit him. He decided to clean up his cabin by throwing all the dirty dishes and clothes behind his cabin. In the spring the snow melted fast and the runoff took all his dirty belongings down to the swollen creek. He spent a few days following the creek picking up his things until he came to the part running behind Bill's and Luther's cabin where the last of his pots, and pans landed. That is how they met and became friends.

Another friend of Bill's and Luther's, Dave ran a trap line and he had the portable butcher shop in the back of his ancient Chevy suburban. Dave's skills provided the elk we enjoyed upon our initial arrival. Dave described an incident where he had been chasing a bear after a shot and a miss. He followed it up near the tree line where he noticed the tracks in the snow had doubled back. The bear stood upright behind a tree waiting for him. He turned around and as he described it, got the hell out of there. The average person would certainly think this was a tall tale or at least a significant exaggeration. But to sit there and to hear him tell it with his slight stutter and with his deep respect for these animals, we couldn't help but believe him.

After a week we decided that as Ben Franklin said "guests, like fish, began to smell after three days." So, we loaded the Jeep and left these wonderful folks some of our bounties. We shared our canned goods just as they had shared their fresh meet. They were extremely grateful, as these were delicacies to people that depended on the land for food. Their lives involved as much famine as it did feast.

It was time for us to get back on the road after John and Debbie said their goodbyes.

British Columbia, Canada

We drove back through Eureka and continued north, crossing the border on highway 93 in Roosville, British Columbia near the Tabacco Plains Indian Reservation No. 2.

We stopped for inspection after crossing into Canada and filled out the proper papers with all the declarations we had to claim. The inspector started to search the Jeep from top to bottom. He was not pleased with the gas cans or the fact we brought our engine oil. He was also concerned with all the food we had. This was not normal for the average tourist visiting their country. He seemed to have a personal mission to make sure every vehicle that he inspected would spend an appropriate amount of money in Canada and our situation led him to believe we were an obstacle to that goal. After he finished, he asked us if we had any other items to declare. He maybe should have looked at our declaration list we just filled out.

When we told him about the shotgun, 303 British Enfield, 22 caliber rifles, and the 30-30 Winchester. He must have wondered where we put the guns. How in the hell could he have missed them, probably most important, were any of his buddies watching? This was a Jeep they searched for a good ten minutes. All he could do after that was to tag all the guns and send us on our way, with a stern warning not to break the seals. There would be other checkpoints on the way, but somehow, we were not worried.

After driving for several hours, we needed to get gas, or now that we are in Canada, petrol. On the roads we now traveled, there are not as many service stations as we expected. So, when we saw one, even if we had half a tank, we pulled out the map and to see how far it was to the next town.

As we pulled into the petrol stations, the only difference we noticed was unfamiliar names like Petro-Canada a crown corporation of Canada, or a state-owned enterprise. We also saw familiar names like Sunoco and Esso, and Texaco, just to name a few. But there was also something else different, the price on the sign was cheap, really cheap. But when we looked closer, we realized it paid for liters, not gallons.

Back in our last year of high school teachers introduced the metric system to us and told us this was the future and we will have to learn the new system. Thank you, President Jimmy Carter. What we didn't know was it had spread to Canada too. In early April of 1975, a Sunoco gas station at the corner of Toronto's Jarvis and Isabella streets introduced the motoring public to the new way of paying for gasoline. Rather than cents per gallon (54.5) it would now be cents per liter (14.4) and his station was the first in the country to do so.

They were also having their gas war just like in the states. So, when the sign went up displaying the new pricing system no one read the small print above the price, and cars lined up for blocks thinking this was some type of publicity stunt and they wanted in on it. For most of the people, it didn't matter because they requested gas by the dollar, not the gallon. This made no sense until they realized two dollars' worth of gas ran out four times as fast as it did before the "promotion."

The Canadian government ordered companies to implement something they called "metrication." This included, over the next few years, Fahrenheit to Celsius, and miles per hour (mph) to kilometers per hour (km/h). The gas companies were the first to start the changeover. Maybe they thought there was a way to make a buck through the confusion? There were quite a few independent stations that held out for some time, refusing to change until they were forced to do so.

As we pulled up to the pumps a guy in maybe his mid-thirties, in familiar attendant coveralls, walked up to us and said 'filler up?' As he was topping off the tank, we stretched our legs and asked if they took traveler's cheques. Sure do, he said, with an odd smile. John grabbed some Navy Player Canadian cigarettes as we were out of our smokes, and that's all they had. We counter-signed in front of him and he handed us our change in Canadian dollars and off we went. Just like in the States. He knew we would soon discover that there was one step missing.

Everything was going very well in Canada until we went to fill up the next time. Everything was the same, fill er up, traveler's cheques but when it was time for the change he said "Oh, these are US dollars," and went inside to get the conversion rate? This was the first time we traveled outside the USA so we were not familiar with "conversion rates" and had no idea what he meant. Turns out the US dollar went a little farther than the Canadian dollar by 1USD = 0.97CAD. Not much but it all adds up.

As we pulled away, we started talking about our newfound wealth. That's when we realized the last gas, station ripped us off. So much for all Canadians being honest, maybe it's just gas stations we have to watch out for. Turns out this was not the norm, but there were a few stations that did not want to take traveler's cheques. Those mostly had younger attendants that did not know how to use them and the manager or owner was not around. So, in those cases, we made sure we had paper money to use. Besides, we were running out of traveler cheques.

We knew that we had a long drive ahead of us to get to our final destination "the ranch" so Jim mentioned a place his grandfather worked at when he was younger. He even had a picture of Lake Louise. It looked beautiful; the perfect place for a break; about six and a half hours from the border. If everything went, well we should get there in time for a late lunch.

Surprisingly the drive from Roosville to Radium Hot Springs (a name that's stranger than fiction) on 93/95 was mostly agricultural and uneventful.

When we made the turn on to where 93 splits, we started to see the mountains in the distance. They looked so far away but in reality, we'd be at their base in just a few hours. Within minutes of the split, we entered Banff National Park. Just like the customs officer said when we crossed the border, the park ranger checked our vehicle and made sure the tags were still on the guns. He attached his lead-seal tag, by squeezing an imprint of the national park logo on it. This time we were told if we have to shoot something in self-defense, we better bring it to the next checkpoint. As we were pulling away, we joked, what if it was a human? We better tie them to the hood. After all, we didn't want to get in any trouble.

We drove the curvy switchback road of 93 (Kootenay Highway / Banff-Windermere Highway) along the Kootenay River and through the Kootenay National Park. This part of the drive was everything we imagined; from everything we read or pictures we looked at. Every turn brought us deeper into the Rocky Mountains. It's not like, the Badlands in the Dakoda's, these were the true mountains that books were written about and movies portrayed. When we drove through Vermilion Pass, we crossed the Continental Pass east into Alberta.

The turn-on 1/93 or the Trans-Canada Highway brought us along the Bow River on the right. Just past that, we followed the

Bow Valley Pkwy and the rail line. These were here well before 1/93 was even thought of. We were now at the base of the mountains we saw earlier. This part of the drive was good but it was a major divided highway so things seemed to go by a little faster, even though we still were only going about thirty-five miles per hour. Every so often we would go under an overpass that went nowhere. It took the second or third one before we realized they were built for the wildlife. It must be pretty dangerous traveling at night through these remote areas.

Lake Louise, Alberta

We took the ramp to Lake Louise Drive and started to look for a gas station in the resort town of Lake Louise. It has been a long time since a fill-up and driving in the mountains can burn more fuel than expected. With a full tank and the cans topped off, it was on to the lake and resort.

Our hearts were beating hard with the anticipation of what we were about to see but, the Lake Louise Drive was going on for what seemed like forever. After the third major turn, we arrived. The crowning jewel of Lake Louise, the Fairmont Chateau Lake Louise! As listed in the books.

At an elevation of 1540 meters, Lake Louise Village is Canada's highest town, and the community formed around the Chateau Lake Louise sits at 1731 meters. Lake Louise is world-famous for its turquoise lakes, the Victoria Glacier, soaring mountain backdrop, palatial hotel, and incredible hiking and skiing.

But, how did Lake Louise start in the middle of nowhere? After all, this was not an easy place to find, let alone a hundred years ago. Here is a little history we learned from their travel brochure.

Located in Alberta, Canada, Fairmont Chateau Lake Louise is more than a grand luxury hotel; it is a major part of Canada's colorful history. The hotel itself has beginnings with the naming and colonization of Lake Louise. While employed by the Canadian Pacific Railway in 1882, Thomas Wilson was procuring equipment for construction when he heard the sounds of a nearby avalanche. His native companions informed him the sounds were coming from the "snow mountains above the lake." They took him there on horseback and what he saw, he named Emerald Lake because of its blue and green water.

In 1890, Canadian Pacific Railway general manager Cornelius Van Horne had a one-story log cabin constructed on the shore of Lake Louise. This small log cabin had one central area that was used as a dining room, office, bar, and gathering room, as well as a kitchen and two small bedrooms. He called it "Chalet Lake Louise" which hosted visitors from various stations along the railway line. While just 50 guests stayed in 1890, by 1912, that number had risen to 50,000. Despite two fires, his tiny cabin would become today's Fairmont Chateau, Lake Louise. In August 1896, American lawyer Philip Abbot fell to his death while climbing Mount Lefroy. His was the first recorded death from mountaineering in North America. His unfortunate death influenced the Canadian Pacific Railway to hire two professional Swiss mountain guides for the safety of visitors wishing to reach the summit. These guides taught thousands of visitors and locals to mountain climb and ski for the next 55 years.

Due to the rise in popularity of mountain climbing, people began to holiday at Lake Louise for this act, as well as horseback riding, stargazing, and more. Considered the "Hollywood North," many early films were shot at Lake Louise with stars such as John Barrymore, Betty Grable, and Carmen Miranda. Stars also visited in droves including Mary Pickford, Douglas Fairbanks, Alfred Hitchcock, Marilyn Monroe. The 1940s brought WWII and Fairmount Chateau Lake Louise closed to the public. However, Lake Louise was still used by scientists from the Universities of Alberta, Saskatchewan, and Manitoba to develop the Pykrete. The Pykrete is difficult to shatter and slow to melt mixture of wood pulp and ice, which was intended to be used as a tool of war to create floating ice platforms for equipment transport. It was scrapped in favor of faster techniques.

Besides skiing, the area became popular for other adventures. Locals and guests began carving the logging trails and flying over jumps at Tunnel Mountain in the 1920s. Full-scale ski areas were in operation by the 1930s. This caused Fairmount Chateau Lake Louise to open the resort year-round during the peak winter holiday seasons in the 1970s. This eventually led to the 1988 Calgary Winter Olympics being held in Banff National Park. Today, Fairmont Chateau Lake Louise hosts the Lake Louise World Cup every November for winter sports enthusiasts far and wide.

As we walked up to the lake and turned to face the Chateau. It was perfectly placed on the northeast corner of a turquoise glacier-fed lake. Jim started talking about how his grandfather was a chef at the hotel in 1910. This was just before the now Fairmont Chateau Lake Louise had opened so, he was probably instrumental in setting up how the kitchen could serve over 55,000 meals per year. He pulled the photo of the lake from the Chateau that his grandfather had taken back when he was there. And it was amazing for us to see the same scene 65 years later with the only difference being bigger trees. Jim made it a point to get in the same spot for a duplicate picture.

The lake was, pristine, with the thick smell of the pine forest surrounding the lake. As our eyes went up from the lake following the steep slope to bright white snow glacier, we couldn't help but be in awe. We spent the day wandering the area taking in the sights and sounds of the resort, as well as the small town of Lake Louise, adjacent to the Chateau grounds.

Here in the Lake Louise area as we have experienced other locations of amazement and special natural beauty. Everyone was very respectful of where they were and who was around them. It was almost like being in church.

Quesnel, British Columbia

While on 93 north to Jasper we could not help but talk about what we just saw and experienced, what it would have been like to be there one hundred years ago, to see the undisturbed surroundings that were here thousands of years before men were here. Soon, we thought that's going to be us. Walking on an uncut path through the mountains. That's when we saw a camper pulled over on the side of the road. Did the motorist need help, we wondered?

There was not much traffic. We couldn't remember the last time we saw a car or a truck. We were in deep daydreams of all the what if's of where we just were. And now, just like that, we were back to reality.

We learned that we had to be careful of who we trusted. We were inclined to trust everyone but, like the gas station attendant who failed to give us the exchange rate for our dollars, we couldn't be gullible. Back home, there were stories of motorists pretending to be broken down and if you pulled over to help, they robbed you or worse.

We had apprehensions about pulling over to help. But we were in the middle of nowhere. What to do? What to do? As we got closer, we noticed that the driver, a man, maybe in his late thirties was under the hood looking at the steam coming from the engine. This did not look like something foul and then a little girl and her mom came out of the camper to see how the man was doing. The odd thing was, no one was trying to wave us to stop. We slowed down, yes, slower than thirty-five miles per hour, and stopped in front of their camper.

They just stood there and did not say anything. Well, we guessed it's up to us to start. No need to start with the hello's or how are you. Let's just get to the point. We asked if we could help. The look on the lady's face was like a heavy burden was just lifted. The little girl looked up at her mom for approval to be around strangers. After all, we were scruffy-looking teenagers with long hair. Not the typical type of people that would pull over to help someone. Who knows, maybe they thought we were going to do them harm. The man said his engine overheated and asked if we had any water to spare? This we had and pulled out a jug of water. Jim was quick to stop the guy from just pouring the water into the overheated engine. He could crack the block with the cold water. Jim told the guy to start the engine and pour the water in slowly until filled up. Jim was very careful not to say any of this where his wife could hear, you know, to protect his manhood. After it was topped off and the radiator cap was back on and the hood was closed, he signaled to his wife that he had fixed the problem. He was her hero and she smiled.

We told them that we could not drive more than thirty-five miles per hour, so we would follow them until we got to the next town, just in case. The man reached for his wallet. We cut him off before he could say anything. We thought it could have been us in the same situation. We said we were just glad to help. As they were pulling farther and farther away, we could see the little girl in the back window waving at us, and we could not get over how good we felt helping out someone who did not ask for help.

To keep on schedule, we sometimes had to drive late into the night. On one of these occasions, it was well past the normal hours of park operation. We assumed that all staff and rangers were long gone to their homes for the evening. So, we just drove in nice and slow, lights off, and followed the one-way road that was very common in the states.

After about four or five minutes we found a site that looked promising. A few trees set back just a little and just past a tight curve that headlights would not shine on. We pulled in and shut off the engine and just stood there looking for campfire lights, and listening for signs of campers. Nothing. Maybe everyone in Canada turns in early. So far so good. We joked that maybe if we got up early, we could pack up and just leave and save some money. It's not something we planned on doing, but there was no after-hours check-in box or a way to let anyone know we were there. So, we thought we would just play it by ear. We quietly and quickly set up camp and fell asleep even quicker.

When we woke up, we were looking at one of the most breathtaking views anyone could imagine. We were in a magical hidden valley, with huge mountain peaks that were so sharp, you could shave on them. All around us we saw picturesque snow-covered peaks. We did not get up as early as we had hoped, but without a word, we quickly and quietly began to break camp.

We had about half of the Jeep packed up when the ranger stopped by. You could tell this wasn't his first time talking to someone that might be trying to leave without paying. He knew we came in late and did not want to disturb us because it was so late. We had no idea where he was or if he had a cabin around the entrance somewhere. He looked over at our license plate and said "you boys sure did come a long way". We said we sure did; we have been on the road since the middle of June. He looked a little startled, took a second look at our plates. "Illinois,

USA, I thought you were from Alberta. They look almost the same.".

He then proceeded to pull out a pad of papers that looked like a police ticket book. He flipped it open and started to write in it. We thought we were getting a citation of some sort but no, it was a campsite tag. He handed us the tag and said that will be two dollars, Canadian. Since we just paid for the site, there was no need to leave early and we decided to cook up a nice breakfast. And take in the view. With the aroma of fresh coffee now in the air, nearby campers were starting to come out of their travel homes to see who was up so early or, possibly, who had coffee on the cooktop.

Just into our second cup of coffee one of our new neighbors came out from the dense woods dividing the campsites and said "I heard you met Ranger Liam." He introduced himself as William.

It turned out the ranger made rounds before sunrise. More than likely part or all of the two dollars went toward his employment so he was not going to let a latecomer slip by. It was all good and we were happy to not have to rush back on the road.

William was a talker and a nice guy. We could tell he was a knowledgeable traveler and probably recently retired. He sure had the gift of gab, but he knew when to listen. He kept an eye on our cooking progress and just as it finished cooking said "I better get going and see what my wife was up to."

It was kind of creepy but just after we finished cleaning up and breaking down camp, William returned. At this point, we didn't care and still were in no hurry to get on the road. We were both sitting on the same side of the picnic table just looking at the view, still in awe. Our site overlooked the small lake just a short way from us. It was probably a collection pond from the mountain runoff that led into an overflowing river. We must have said something like there must be fish in there or something, because William said, "you should give it a try."

Jim said that was one thing we did not bring with us and we also did not have fishing licenses. With that William said he would be right back and disappeared into the woods. About two minutes later he came back and presented us with a fishing pole and tackle and said now all you need was a license. We said we didn't have any money to give him for the gear and he said it was a gift from one camper to another. We thanked him and told him we could not do it here but we would surely use it soon. He smiled and disappeared into the woods.

We were all packed up and just checking the oil in the Jeep when Liam walked up to say goodbye and asked how we liked our stay in his campground. We said it was wonderful and were sorry for coming in so late last night. He then said he noticed that we met William and asked if he told us what happened to him. We both looked at each other before Liam said, "didn't think so, He's not that type of person." Liam told us that he was robbed a few days ago and they took all his fishing gear, poles, and tackle except for a small pole and a little tackle box behind his seat in his truck. We did not tell him what William did but here was another example of the camping family. We never did use the gift but it meant a lot to us.

The drive to Quesnel would bring us to the farthest westerly point in our planned route. The closer we got to Quesnel, the further we were getting out of the deep Rockies and into the foothills. That might sound like small hills, almost flat but, they are mountains in their own right. The full view of the Rockies was beautiful with the sun hitting the western slope of each peak. We felt kind of sad to be leaving the awesome views that greeted us each morning and tucked us into our sleeping bags each night.

With this new view, we also could see that some of the slopes looked like they were burnt from a fire. Now forest fires are not an uncommon thing up in this vast forest, they are pretty common. Most, well fifty percent, of the fires in the western part of Canada are caused by lighting. Unfortunately, the rest are caused by man. It's kind of hard to tell how long ago a fire might have been. The only way to tell is by the tree growth. But from where we now where we could see a history of fires like a patchwork quilt of scars on the earth.

These were small fires compared to the largest fire in Canada's history, which was man-made. The Chinchaga fire or Wisp fire took place just north-north-east of where we were, in the summer and early fall of 1950 burned a total of 7,700,000 acres. To this day it is the single largest recorded fire in North American History. One reason it was so big was that authorities allowed the fire to burn freely, following local forest management policy. The Authorities based their decision to let it burn partly on the fact that there were not many settlements in the region. There was so much smoke from this fire that it created what was known as the "1950 Great Smoke Pall." People across eastern North America and Europe could see the Pall. At the time, it was not widely publicized because the smoke was mostly in the upper atmosphere and could not be smelled. This also created the world's largest smoke layer in the atmosphere. All that and, it was started by people building a fire to keep insects off their horses.

The Road to the Ranch, British Columbia

We rolled through Quesnel, a small industrial-looking town with uniform streets reminiscent of the railhead town Rapid City, South Dakota, which we passed several weeks before. Quesnel had none of the typical modernization. No chain restaurants or stores of Rapid City.

On the corner of the main street was a collection of Indians from the Chilcotin tribe we assumed, they sat like something right out of a John Wayne movie: wrapped in heavy dark wool blankets; flat-brimmed cowboy hats with feathers sticking out of the hatbands.

We could see the stockyards as we left the center of town, a collection of fences and gates that looked like an unkempt maze, it was empty but was heavily used at certain times of the year. The skies seemed large, and the rolling hills went on forever.

We stopped at a small general store as we passed on our way out of town and picked up some cigarette tobacco as we got nauseous from the Navy Players we picked up in Jasper. Plus, the warning label on the pack told us not to inhale as they had fiberglass in them. We decided to use Prince Albert in a can and get some rolling papers to avoid the Canadian cigarettes.

Taking the road north we began following the Frasier River. The Frasier was a muddy boiling stretch of water weaving its way through the rolling sod-covered foothills. After an hour of driving in which we rechecked our directions many times. We finely came to the road described in our directions that Stan sent us as the road leading to the ranch.

Jim abruptly jerked the wheel to the right on the switchback road and we thundered onto a gravel washboard road that was at a steep incline. We could see the tan-colored swirling torrent that was the Frasier River coming closer on our left as we rumbled down the gravel to an abrupt halt behind a pickup truck and what was left of an old Ford LTD station wagon that had seen better days. There were so many parts missing from the car it was hard to make out the make let alone the model. The occupants of the LTD had a sort of picnic spread laid out in the middle of the gravel. By the looks of this, they knew how long it was going to take to get across.

We stepped out of the Jeep and walked up the bank a bit to see why everything was at a standstill. Just passed the LTD we saw a dock. We guessed that a ferry must run cars across the river. We walked down to the river and saw the ferry about halfway across moving toward the other side at a snail's pace with one car perched on the deck.

The ferry was an interesting affair; it was a row of pontoons running parallel to the river. A cable that stretched across the river was attached with cables and pulleys to both sides of the ferry. To move the ferry, the captain in the pilothouse turned a wheel. Which would shorten one cable causing the boat to move off parallel. The churning river rushed between the pontoons pushing the ferry across.

Stopping about one and a half car lengths back, a Ford one and a half-ton pickup truck pulled in behind us. Two guys jumped out and walked down to us. The driver, Lenny, was a tall curly-haired fellow wearing dungarees and a dark green uniform shirt. Kent, a guy with blond hair and a blond goatee, jumped out of the passenger side Kent hollered in a thick British accent, 'how long you chaps been waiting. Lenny explained that they worked for the forestry service; Kent was a sort of exchange student from the UK and Lenny had been working summers for the forestry department for a couple of years.

We were talking with them for a few minutes when a beat-up old stake bed pickup truck, came rumbling down the hill and pulled in front of the forestry truck, and slid to a stop just behind our Jeep Inside were about five or six people. Kent immediately ran back to the window of the truck and began complaining to the driver about cutting in line. Lenny got a little flushed, and slowly shrunk in front of our Jeep to be less noticeable to the occupants of the truck. He quietly explained to us that the people in the truck were members of a local Indian tribe, that had the reputation of cutting the throats of anyone who crossed them the wrong way. Lenny explained that they have what they call a "tribal enforcer" that accomplishes his charge when he is ready and that can take several weeks or even months from the time the tribe is crossed. Kent didn't know any better and would probably get cut if he pissed them off.

We looked at each other in amazement. We were as close to the "Wild West" as we could get. Or was Lenny pulling our leg?

Nevertheless, he seemed genuinely concerned. Lenny also told us that there wasn't much on the other side of the river except a few ranches and that most of the traffic was because the Indians were tending their nets. They string nets to catch the abundant fish in the river, a practice that is illegal for anyone except the Indian's, he explained, and a much-disputed agreement with the Canadian government.

We later heard about some guys getting their throats cut by Indians during the "Billy Barker Days" and the "Quesnel Rodeo" and wondered if Kent had been a victim as Lenny had more or less predicted. The Billy Barker Days were the perfect backdrop to conceal any revenge that may need to be handed out. The festival would last about a week and there would be a lot of visitors in and out of the town. You would think that this would have been going on for years but, no it just started in 1973 as a way to, as the council describes it; "Hatched the idea of a summer festival to showcase our beautiful town and its pride in our gold rush heritage to the many visitors stopping in Quesnel." Good for them to try and draw someone to the middle of nowhere.

We finally got our turn and crossed the river. We hopped into the Jeep, we started it by popping the clutch as we rolled the rest of the way down the steep hill toward the ferry. As we crossed. The sun was getting a little lower in the west causing shadows in the swirling river and Jim commented that "I sure wouldn't want to fall in there."

After we pulled off the ferry and drove a couple of hundred feet up the dirt road, we stopped to check our directions. "Stay to the right for three miles, make a quick left at the fork, and then up the driveway about one and a half miles. We continued up the road being careful not to raise too much dust and avoiding as many of the really large potholes as we could. Finally, we came to the fork in the road, it was more like a stone-covered path. We proceeded up the path, which wound up and up through rather dense woods, not large trees, most about as big around as a fence post, but all hardwoods with thick growths of thorn bushes between them.

We eventually came to a clearing broken by several fences. We had a hard time telling if they were set up to keep things in or out. The fence posts seemed to go every which away. Right in the center with a cleared hill rising behind was the ranch house. We had arrived.

The Ranch, British Columbia

The ranch house was a rustic, wood frame single-story structure. A quaint house with a large front porch with a side door. A path wound up around the side of the house for about fifty feet to a door in a hill that housed a heavily used root cellar. Through two diagonal fences and about 300 feet, we saw a small ancient log barn. Next to the barn and on the way to the root cellar was a machine shed full of rusted equipment. Halfway up the hill sat a fifty-five Ford box truck with large chocks under the wheels to prevent it from rolling down the hill. Further up the hill stood another outbuilding also ancient and perched precariously on piles of stone at the front corners in an effort to make it level on the hill. Just behind that, a chicken coop.

As we approached the house a chubby little kid named Larry, about fourteen, ran past us chasing a chicken. A skinny little boy they called Ben, about nine, and a girl named Alice about four followed him. The skinny kid and his sister stopped dead in their tracks at the sight of us before they ran inside the house. The chubby boy kept right on chasing the chicken until he was out of sight behind the barn.

We walked up to the house and onto the covered porch, but before we could knock, the screen door flew open, and out came Stan, John's neighbor's younger brother, and his wife, Judy. They had been expecting us as we had made arrangements through one of John's neighbors to work on the ranch for a few weeks. Stan welcomed us and could tell we were beaten from the long drive. He directed us up the hill to the bunkhouse, the precariously perched, ancient outbuilding up the hill. Stan called for Larry, the chubby boy chasing the chicken who emerged from behind the barn. He told Larry to show us to the bunkhouse and said we could park up by the Ford and get ourselves settled.

Jim drove the Jeep part way up the hill and parked it. As we walked up toward the bunkhouse, we crossed a small creek that came down the hill and across it just in front of the bunkhouse. We looked inside and saw a filthy floor with a sleeping bag near the door on one side and a dilapidated potbelly stove at the far end. Larry began telling us of his winning battle with the mice when he had arrived five weeks earlier.

We decided to clean the place and set up some bunk beds with the pile of old lumber sitting next to the building. After a thorough sweeping, we assembled a platform for Larry and a bunk bed setup for both of us, they were just planked platforms but they would keep us off the floor.

We turned our attention to the stove. Larry screamed don't go near the stove it's full of bees. After careful evaluation, we could see a fair size nest inside the stovepipe. Retrieving some bug repellent from the Jeep we thoroughly soaked the thing and removed it. We cleaned out the stove and reattached the vent pipe that was lying on the floor behind the stove.

We impressed Larry who hadn't thought to sweep the place and had been living in that filth since he had arrived. Larry told us that he was from Vancouver, an inner-city kid, and had never seen a tree outside of a city park before this. On his fourteenth birthday, his grandfather picked him up for an overnight and drove him here. He had made arrangements for Larry to work with Stan the summer. A complete surprise to Larry. His grandfather dropped him off and said he would pick him up after he lost some weight. We kind of felt sorry for Larry, but this didn't last as we got to know him.

After finishing the cleaning of the bunkhouse, we used our tools to construct our beds. It turned out our well-stocked tool chest, equipped for any eventuality was complete enough for this daunting job.

We unloaded the essentials from the Jeep and had ourselves all settled in quickly. The sun moved little in all this time, which seemed curious to us. From our vantage point at the bunkhouse halfway up the hill, we could see several miles in three directions, from open fields to the north followed by trees, treetops to the west heavy woods to the south and beyond them all gently rolling hills. The Rocky Mountains were many miles to the east behind us, up over the hill were several upper cattle ranges.

After some time, Stan came up the hill to see how we were making out and to give us instructions for the following morning. Stan peered in and his jaw dropped, he was amazed at our work on the bunkhouse. Where the hell did you get the tools, he quipped. John said we came prepared. Stan just shook his head with a smile and said, "I will see you in the morning." As he walked back down the hill his entourage of two children followed him back to the ranch house.

Shortly after we had arrived, the skinny kid insisted on showing us his pet rabbit Oscar. He was a large black rabbit that was so fat he could hardly move. The kid said he had been raising him for a couple of years and played with it regularly out of its cage as it was really slow and never tried to run off.

The next morning, we awoke to an incredibly loud pounding, as our heads began to clear from sleep, the first thing we thought of was an earthquake or maybe this old bunkhouse was sliding down the hill. We noticed that Larry was calmly putting his boots on. He looked over at us and said its Stan waking us up for work.

Stan was beating on the door with a 16-ounce claw hammer. John said what the hell its 4:00 AM. And, the sun was halfway to the middle of the sky; the same position we felt like it was in when we went to sleep.

We worked our way down the hill and Stan was there waiting for us. He said someone left the gate open last night so you will have to get the horses and then come in for breakfast. The skinny kid Ben was milking an elderly dairy cow next to the barn and Stan told Larry to take Alice and get some eggs from the chicken coop.

John and Jim started chasing the horses around the yard. This was very frustrating because just as you got close enough to touch one, they would again bolt out of reach. Over and over, we repeated this until we finally developed a method to snag them.

Stan had three horses: a Black quarter horse named Ben, a Tan Buck named Brownie, and another Quarter horse named Star. Once they were secure, we went inside for breakfast.

The kitchen was a large eat-in affair with a giant round table on one end with an equally gargantuan lazy Susan sitting in the middle. Stan's wife Judy was saying to him, "Do you think this milk is still good from last year?" Stan replied sure it is, it's been frozen for a year. Stan explained that last year the cow, Ethel, was a real producer so they froze several gallons. Stan commented on how she is showing her age and they get very little milk anymore. At any rate, the whole conversation was not too appetizing for a couple of guys from the suburbs.

Stan began filling glasses with the yellow lumpy stuff, as he did, he asked John and Jim if we would like a glass, we both quickly declined politely, who would have known that lumpy stuff was cream? Larry came in the back door with a bucket of water with about two dozen eggs in it. Judy hollered "What have you done! I told you to get a few eggs" Larry replied "I got them all."

The ones on the right side of the coup were fertile, and for god's sake why did you put them in water. Larry replied sheepishly that they were less likely to break that way. He whined how sorry he was because he didn't know better. Judy told us to sit down to breakfast. Before our butts hit the chairs, the lazy Susan began turning as the kids and Stan scooped out big portions of the three homemade apple pies Judy just made for breakfast. We each were able to manage a small piece before there was nothing left on the table.

After breakfast, we asked Stan what was planned for the day and he said we will be doing some haying but first some of the neighbors' cattle had managed to get into the field and had to be herded out. Stan asked Larry to direct us down to the "first lower field" after we cleaned up and got our gloves.

We pulled the top off the Jeep and started down the road toward the lower field the way Larry showed us. When we arrived, we found a long hayfield surrounded by thick woods and bordered on one side by the road with a gate on one end that was opened and another gate on the far end along the road. The field was a somewhat flat patch of ground on the side of the hill. We could see the cattle milling about in the center.

We decided to go in the far gate and use the Jeep to drive the cattle out the other, thereby impressing our new employer with our skill and ingenuity. No need to ask Stan how this should be done, with so obviously a solution at hand. So, we continued up the road and quietly entered the far gate. We began driving hard for the cattle beeping the horn and shouting just like a Roy Rogers episode, except a Jeep instead of a trusty horse like Trigger. Our plan worked. The cattle ran toward the open gate Suddenly Stan's dog, a large German shepherd, appeared at the gate barking ferociously. The cattle turned and ran into the thick woods at the end of the field. Just as the cattle disappeared into the woods, Stan came running up from another field further down the hill, He was furious with us for our misguided attempt at driving the cattle. Stan demanded the driver's seat and headed for the low end of the woods that the cattle were snarled up in. He double-clutched the Jeep and did it like an old pro. He scolded us on the way shouting "those ain't F'n Wisconsin dairy cows," the reality of which we were soon to learn.

We slowly worked our way along the woods toward the gate. Stan worked them toward the gate slowly as the cattle crashed into everything, the fence, the trees, and the Jeep. The skinny kid showed up on horseback and began driving the strays back into the crowd and eventually worked them through the gate. At one point we began getting out of the Jeep to help drive them on foot, and Stan screamed are you nuts they will kill you. This was just the beginning of our education on the differences between cows, and range cattle.

We spent the rest of the day in another field slightly farther up the hill disassembling irrigation pipes and stacking them on a trailer to be moved to another field. After some simple instruction from Stan, he was gone. Maybe this was supposed to be some form of punishment for the cow thing, who knows? Each piece of pipe was three-inch in diameter aluminum, twenty feet long with couplings on each end. The section of pipe weighed just over forty pounds. The first few sections weren't so bad. Grab it in the middle, put on your shoulder, adjust and all you had to do was walk it to the trailer. Piece of cake. Until you started to get further and further away. Then that section would start to bounce. Just a little at first. Then with each step, the bounce would multiply until it would almost jump off your shoulder. After a few of these "near bounce offs" we got the steps down and were making good time and finished the entire field just as Stan was coming back to check on us. He didn't say a good job or, you did it all wrong. Just, it's time to eat. As we returned to the house, we were amazed at the fact that it was still light out at 10:00 P.M.

We were getting pretty hungry about then because we did not stop for lunch, so when the call for dinner was made, we quickly found our spots around the table. The meal consisted of a large pot of soup with a ladle sticking out and a small loaf of bread. Again, the lazy Susan began its spin and these people were fast. By the time we could grab the ladle there was just enough soup left to half fill our bowl while tipping the pot. After the hard day we had put in we were still ravenous.

We went back to the bunkhouse and dug into our canned goods for a little canned stew. The only way to heat it was to fire up the old potbelly stove. We did reassemble it but, never tested it. Well, no time like the present. We still had some wood in the Jeep, so we brought in a few pieces and split them into small, fast to light, and faster to burn pieces. In no time the top was hot enough to make a late-night snack. Just enough to get us through the night. Oh, and Larry watched us from start to finish and never said a word. Probably because he ate most of the soup and maybe, just maybe he felt a little guilty. We turned in about 11:30 with the sun just setting through the window.

The next morning, we again were awakened to Stan's claw hammer. With a single piece of pie, we were sent to one of the hayfields Stan used to feed his cattle over the winter, this time we were instructed on the cutting, raking, baling and stooking (stacking on end so the rain will not soak the hay) of hay. John pulled the swather (the cutter that also forms the cut hay into a windrow) behind an old International Harvester tractor while Larry and Jim proceeded down to the lower field on foot to stack hay Stan had already cut.

Stan thought John should be the one who should be driving and operating the tractor. We don't know where he got that idea from but from that point on, that was John's job.

John's instruction began with the tractor. Every day he said, the first thing is to check the oil and gas and fill as needed. Then fill the jug with oil and put it in the box mounted behind the seat with all the other essential supplies and tools, this included a gallon of water for the tractor or you. Whoever needed it first. Then he asked if John ever drove a tractor before and he said no. Stan said, "well you drove a Jeep across North America and that should be good enough." With that John's tractor training was over and Stan moved on to the equipment.

Pretty simple, the cutter/swather, the rake, and the baler. Each piece had a different task and challenges like making sure the cutting blades were not banged up and were as sharp as could be with the file in the box. The rake had long wires around five wheels set at Pretty simple, the cutter/swather, the rake and the baler. Each piece had different tasks and challenges like making sure the cutting blades were not banged up. The rake had to be set at a forty-five-degree angle that would turn the cut rows over to dry. The baler had to have twine to tie the bales together, oddly a fresh spool of twine was 5000 feet and that made us laugh, thinking back to our survival instructor Ben and our first day of survival class. But most importantly John had to make sure there was plenty of sheer pins in the box. "What the hell are those for," he asked. Stan just said he would know when to use them.

John got the tractor all ready to go, hooked up the swather to the PTO (power take-off) on the tractor, and followed everyone down the road in first gear. There was no point in going any faster due to all the pot-holes. Stan got Jim and Larry started on stooking a field that had been cut and dried days ago, this is making small clusters of hay to continue the drying process.

John admitted sweet relief that he didn't have that job. Stan said to follow him in first gear through a field and down a long path to a huge field. I sure wish I had a camera. This was amazing. The field went down a 4/12 pitch (for every 12 inches of distance there is a drop of four inches) slope about a mile, give or take, with the Fraser River about fifty feet past the end of his field. This was about nine hundred yards wide with a tree line on each side. There was a slight breeze blowing the soon-to-be-cut hay. It looked like ocean waves rolling across the entire field. I shut off the tractor and got into the Jeep.

We took a drive around the hay fields I was going to be working in and Stan told John what were his and which were his neighbors, and the way he wanted the fields to be worked. Just to give an idea of the size of some of these fields, Stan owned 3000 acres. We could not see across to the other side of any of his fields. He owned 150 head of range cattle and we never saw any of them. So, working in any field was going to be an all-day task. He then drove John back to where the tractor was and left him to get started.

John knew he had to start in the gear you wanted to work in. And after looking at the job at hand and what time it was, he decided third gear would get the whole field cut and he could get back while there was still daylight. So, he pushed in the clutch, shifted into third, gear and let the clutch out slowly. Not bad, throttled up and went to turn around to start cutting parallel with the slope. That's when he saw the rock. He turned downhill to avoid hitting it and now was heading straight downhill, gaining speed. The swather was bouncing all over the place and parts were falling out of the box behind the seat. He put the throttle all the way down but by this time it did not slow down at all. All he could think about was trying to explain to Stan how his tractor ended up in the Frasor River!

Well, throttling down did not work so next was to downshift. This would surely slow me down. Out of third and into first here we go. Clutch in, out of gear, and, oh no. There is no synchronizer in the transmission to get into first. That's why you start in the gear you want to work in. Ok, deep breath, freewheeling down a hill, hit the brakes. John never tried them until that very moment. Maybe he should have because they did not work! On-farm tractors there is a right and left rear wheel brake that you can lock together during on-the-road driving. This way you could not hit one break and swing into another lane or off the road. They were not locked. If the brakes did work, he might have rolled the tractor. Again, that would require more explaining to Stan how he destroyed his tractor. At about this time John was running out of ideas when he remembers skiing in Colorado on slopes that look just like this. Switchback, of course, he slowly turned and after a few seconds was perpendicular with the slope and rolled to a stop in twenty feet. He shut off the tractor and got off and looked uphill. He only traveled about five hundred feet but, it felt like a half mile. He sure wishes that jug of water was full of beer, he could have used one about that time.

Back up to the top, but this time in first gear, John set up to start cutting, and away he went. Not too bad, a little slow at first but he determined not to have a repeat of what he just went through. First pass, great, made the turn without a problem. So, what if it takes me three days to cut this. Well, maybe he should try second gear. After all, the first gear was pretty slow. Second pass and turn, all good. John was in his comfort zone; he could do this all day... and then, can you believe it, John hit that stupid rock. The same one he tried to avoid when he barreled down the hill in third gear. No damage but what the hell! He stopped and picked up the rock and put it in the box behind the seat. Not going to run over that with the other equipment he thought.

Then he found another and another. This is going to be a long day but he planned to keep going with his eyes open, for sure. When he got to the tree line on either side, he would just throw the rocks into the trees. This would be every four or five passes but at least it might save a future breakdown.

Stan came out around lunchtime and brought me a gallon of water and a piece of apple pie. This turned out to be a regular activity depending on the fruit that was available that day. John said that he started to look forward to this delivery service. Stan was probably just checking on John and was happy to see that the job was much further along than expected. Stan had no idea what John went through with the tractor and the hill. He did see a box full of rocks and asked what John was doing with them. He had plenty of shear pins and John should not waste time stopping to clear rocks. John still didn't know what the shear pins were for but guessed he'd find out sooner or later.

Larry was a lazy character and was difficult to work with. As soon as Stan was out of sight, he stopped doing anything. Jim found himself, nagging, badgering, and threatening him to get him moving. Stooking bails is hard work. It consisted of gathering bails that were randomly deposited by the baler and creating small stacks of three, four, and five bails each arranged in such a way to continue to dry with the grain of the top bail set to shed water in the event of rain.

After a very long day, we made our way back to the ranch house to find Stan waiting for us with the horses. You guys will have to take turns, as we don't have enough saddles, Stan said as we walked up. Stan asked us to herd some cattle down the road to the neighbor's place. He told us not to get fancy and let the horses do the work because they knew what they were doing and we didn't. Stan was right, the horses went right to work the moment we came upon the herd. They went back and forth moving the cattle down the road and went after strays that headed into the bush, all we had to do was hold on and duck low branches. The underbrush tore up our legs and from that point on we made sure we wore the chaps that Stan had offered that were hanging in the shed. After several hours of this, and bareback besides, we knew why John Wayne walked the way he did.

After we ate dinner that night, we went up to the bunkhouse to kick back and rest. It was a long hard day and Larry was being Larry. Just a pain in the ass. If we asked him a question, he would say "I don't know." Or if we asked him to help with something he would say "I'm busy," or some other smart-aleck remark. For some reason tonight, it was getting to both of us.

When Jim asked Larry where his hat was. Larry said if you would put it away, you would know where it was. And, at that point, Jim knew he did something with it. That was it. John could feel it in the air. Kind of like just before it starts to rain. It's windy, then it gets real calm, and the air has that fresh ozone smell to it. Then a few seconds later all hell breaks loose. But this time, it was like just before lighting hits! Have you ever been close to a lightning strike? All your hair seems to stand up just before the explosion

Jim was on the top bunk with a "strikes anywhere" match in his teeth; Positioned kind of like a toothpick, just there without a purpose. John knew when Jim did this he was in a relaxed state of mind and not much could get him stirred up, except Larry.

Jim said, "what did you just say," and jumped down off the bunk and landed hard on the floor with a loud thud. John thought the building was going to fall off the rocks holding it up. But it didn't. Jim was now standing about two feet from Larry and John knew Jim wanted to knock some sense into him but, sometimes, in the words of some country singer, you just can't fix stupid.

Through this whole scene John sat on the lower bunk bed sharping his knife. It was nothing special. A four-inch Barlow folding knife with imitation plastic grips. He had it for a long time and broke the tip off. After an hour or so with a metal file, the tip was almost good as new, just a little shorter. Somewhere along the line, he chipped one of the grips throwing it. Not in anger, he just liked to throw it. He would set up boards in the backyard at home or throw them at trees or things on the ground. After a few years of doing this, John was pretty good at hitting what he aimed at. Well, most of the time. After all, he did break the tip off and he did chip the handle.

So, back to Jim and Larry. Larry must have been able to get away with a lot back home but, he was here now. Larry said, "what are you going to do about it?"

Jim took the match out of his mouth and threw it at Larry. It bounced off his chest and landed on the floor right in-between his feet. I saw a target and let the knife fly from where I was sitting, about eight feet away. The knife tip stuck deep in the floor just, grazing the tip of the match fizzing to a blue-yellow flame and filling our tiny room with the smell of sulfur. Holy shit, there's no way John could ever do that again in a million years.

The look on Larry's face was priceless. Kind of like an ah-ha life-changing moment. Jim, without saying a word just reached over and picked up the lit match and with the other hand pulled the knife out of the floor. He lit a cigarette, flicked the match out, closed the knife, and handed, slow and easy, back to John. Jim said to Larry, "I'm not the one you should worry about." Larry pulled Jim's hat out from behind some wood and said I'm sorry. That moment might have changed his life forever.

After halfway into our second week Stan, wanted us to stack up some of the hay bales that were ready to store up by the barn. I think he was just looking for something to keep us busy while he and Judy went into town. Judy just started working at a local newspaper part-time (We think they were running short of money,) and Stan was going to try to work a deal for a hay sale with locals in town. Both were not expected back until dinner time. The real downside was we had to keep an eye on all the kids!

Stan gave very specific instructions on putting hay in the barn and where he wanted the hay stacked outside by the barn. He must have had a forty-foot by forty-foot tarp because that is the footprint he wanted.

We got the farm wagon hooked up to the tractor, topped off the tractor with fluids, and got all the kids together. Two of the kids had runny noses and were drinking out of one jug of water, our only jug of water! We thought it might be better if we got our canteens from the Jeep and used them for ourselves.

We got all the kids on the wagon and Jim hopped on the front of the wagon with his legs hanging over the deck. Jim had a pretty good seat. Farm wagons have pivoting axles in the front and rear. The hitch arm is fixed to the axle so when the arm that is connected to the hitch moves from one side to the other the axle moves in the same direction. This way farmers can hook up more than one wagon and they will all follow in the same path as the tractor. This also means that the wagon will jerk from side to side randomly until you start a turn. This kind of wagon has no side walls, just a flatbed with nothing to hold on to. The kids were pretty accustomed to this setup and did a really good job at not falling off very much.

When we got to our first field, we loaded up the wagon edge to edge, six bales high with the front only four so everyone had a place to sit. The road to the fields had a lot of turns and one sharp switchback up near the house.

The first trip was in first gear and as you can guess took a long time, but we did not lose any bales or people. We started loading the barn first because we thought it was going to hold the most. You know, get the hard work done first.

The second trip was loaded the same way but this time we were in second gear. Not bad, lost one bale on the switchback and no kids. But we did not even put a dent in the field it was so big. So...

On the third trip we loaded the wagon the same way, but this time we tried third gear. The kids started laughing and having a great time. After each turn, the wagon jerked from side to side and the kids thought it was a game even though we lost four or five bales. So, after a while, I could throttle up the gas and make some time. It wasn't until the fifth trip that, along with losing a few bales, we lost one of the kids, Ben. No one told us until after the switchback that he fell off. But the other kids said it happens all the time and no one gets hurt. We could just pick him up on the way back down. Sure enough, there he was sitting on a bale waiting for us.

We had a good system going, and no one was complaining, so we filled the second story of the barn pretty fast. Now on to the stacks beside the barn.

We roughly marked out the forty-by-forty dimensions Stan wanted and made our first layer. It was a little tricky to layout because if the bales were not set correctly the outside bales could fall off. It would have helped if Stan would have shown us this step of bricklaying. Ultimately, they needed to be placed in such a way the hay strands would shed water. With that done we were making a great time with round trips. First, second, third, fourth layer this thing was getting huge. For a while, I could pull the tractor right next to the stack but that did not last. We had to start making steps in the bales to get them to the next level. This got old fast, and we just about had enough when one of their neighbors stopped by. She was an older woman, carrying a 30-06 rifle, we guessed in her 60's, she was gaunt and looked vary weathered. She was strong as an ox and had incredible stamina as we were to find out.

She was very impressed with what we accomplished. When we told her how we got the bales up so far, she said, oh is the hay buck broke? She leaned her rifle against the fence and went into the barn and pulled out a twenty-foot conveyor lift powered by a small gas engine. She gave it a few pulls and it started right up. She looked up at us and said Stan must have forgotten to tell you about it. Not sure about that. But Stan did underestimate how fast we could get things done.

With our newfound tool, and the neighbor pitching in, it was back to work. We finished that load in record time. At one point the neighbor called for a smoke and coffee break, she came prepared with a thermos and cups. Probably Stan asked her to check up on us, while we were enjoying this, she shared a piece of sage wisdom "if we didn't smoke or drink coffee, we would all work ourselves to death."

We wondered why she was carrying the rifle when she arrived, she explained that everyone carries guns for protection from bears and other animals that pose a risk and may even attack the livestock.

Before long the field was almost done except for a few bales on the far side of the field. We picked them up and looked to the west and could see the sky getting dark and a storm was rolling in. We drove up to the house as fast as we could, picking up the last of the bales that fell off. We unloaded and stacked the last of the bales, put the hay buck away, and parked the tractor. A light refreshing rain felt great!

Shortly after we finished, Stan and Judy pulled up with their headlights shining on the haystack. They both got out and just stared at the stack that was almost twenty feet tall. After what seemed like five minutes, Stan said "how the hell did you do that?"

After a hard day of haying and a rough afternoon of herding the neighbor's cattle out of the field and down the road to the next ranch over, John's legs were incredibly sore from holding on to the horse. It was his day to go without a saddle. Stan called us up to the house after we had attended the horses. A friend of his had been by earlier and dropped off several bottles of homemade beer. Stan handed us each a beer and warned us not to drink the sludge in the last half inch of the bottles. He said that the beer was not filtered like store-bought beer and should always settle before drinking or you could get sick, but the beer sure hit the spot.

Leaving British Columbia

The next day we were again up at the crack of dawn after Stan had again pounded on the bunkhouse door with a hammer. We went down to the main house for breakfast, and again the lazy Susan began to spin and this time the breakfast of buttered toast and preserves was nearly gone by the time it reached our side of the table.

Stan sent us to continue haying and tasked us with moving a mile or so of irrigation pipe. As we headed for the compound to put the horses in the corral and clean up the tack, we saw Stan's kid pealing the skin of his pet rabbit as it was time for it to be dinner. Although we were appalled at the site, we understood that on a farm or ranch all the animals are resources. It just seemed odd how happy the kid was to kill his pet. That evening we were called to dinner; it was a pot of rabbit soup. They planned on that small rabbit being a couple of meals. This time the lazy Susan spun and John stopped it and made sure he got a full bowl of soup. The rabbit broth was tasty but not very filling.

After that meal, we knew we had to get out of there before we were starved, or worked to death. We were tired of working till sundown in the land of the midnight sun without enough to eat. We went back to the bunkhouse to discuss our options. We thought of bolting, but that was no good, we wanted to get paid. Jim said what about a sick relative, John said, good who?

186

It can't be one of my relatives, Stan knows my parents. Okay, Jim said, how about my aunt is dying so that we have to be there as soon as possible? Good said John. We will wait for the next letter to arrive and use our excuse to get the hell out of here.

Three days passed and we waited for that letter. Over the last couple of days, Jim repaired an old CJ5 Jeep that Stan had set in a shed for several years. It was a washed-out brown color, which was good since it helped hide the rust and the cancerous holes weren't as noticeable. The only major problem was a U-joint that had popped open spilling needle bearings into the dirt. It must have happened when someone tried to pull it out of the shed because Jim found most of them under the Jeep where it sat. Those he couldn't find got replaced with cut pieces of wire. He also used the wire to fasten as much as possible of the body back to the frame. Jim had that thing held together literally with spit and baling wire.

He filled the Jeep's tires using the old Ford box truck that Stan had. Equipped with an air hose with a hollowed-out spark plug on one end and a filler valve on the other. Removing a spark plug from the flathead V8 engine and replacing it with the hose fitting, Jim started the engine, and voila! Instant air compressor.

Jim drove the CJ5 out to the lower pasture to show Stan. He hit a bump and the battery crashed through the rusted fender and rolled right over to Stan and came to a rest on his foot, but the jeep was still running, and Stan was mighty impressed. Stan was so impressed he asked Jim to take a look at the family car.

The family car was an old 68 Buick Skylark with about two hundred thousand miles on it. The motor was a great old V6 that hadn't run on more than three cylinders in years.

Jim agreed because it sure beats haying. Early the next morning after breakfast he started in on it. He pulled the plugs and after a compression test, found that a valve job on one head ought to do the trick. Stan thought this was great since he was not the least bit mechanically inclined. He was heading for a machine shop the next day and would take the head with him. He could also get the gasket set needed for Jim to reassemble the engine.

The next day a letter came and our plan went into action. That evening, when Stan got back from town, we broke the news to Stan and Judy that we would be leaving in the morning. They were very appreciative of the work we did for them and they paid us double the going rate of $25 a week for 16-hour workday 7 days a week and barely enough food to survive. But we needed every bit of it if we were to continue on our trip. We were there for three weeks and each received a check for $150.00. The $300.00 we now had was going to go a long way!

Jim spent some time explaining to Stan how to reassemble the engine in the Buick until he felt confident, he could do it. Still, Jim figured the Buick just might replace the Jeep in the shed for the next several years.

We said our good-byes and headed back across the Fraiser River and North through the night to the next town on our map: Prince George.

The George Motel

The morning was still, and clear, as we rolled into "Prince George." We decided to cash the checks, from Stan as soon as we made it back to civilization. We pulled into the first Bank we could find. We endorsed our checks and walked up to the teller. We anticipated a little trouble since the checks were on another bank and we had no account here. At first, the teller said no way. As we went into our stranded traveler story she began to break. She told please wait there as she went to get the manager. After a long discussion with one of the 75 bank vice presidents, she returned and told us she would only be allowed to do this one time as if we would come back with the same story.

With our newfound wealth, we decided to be extravagant and get a motel room where we could clean up, not having bathed in about a month. So, we checked into the George Motel and cleaned up. After turning on the TV and getting bored with the single TV channel and the endless farm report that was available, we decided to take a walk around town.

John had wanted to purchase a new pistol ever since Montana, and after our days on the Ranch, we decided to treat ourselves and do a little shopping. At the end of the street, there was a well-stocked gun store, so we went to see if they had a gun for John.

The store had a wide variety of black powder pistols and other accessories. Jim found a large leather ammo belt like Poncho Via wore across his shoulder that held the 30/30 rounds for his Winchester, and John found a mighty sweet looking 44 Cal Navy Colt, cap and ball pistol.

We were discussing our concerns about bringing guns back across the border when the store owner said "No sweat I'll ship it to you anywhere." We looked at each other and nodded. Can you ship it "General Delivery Manistique Michigan?" Sure, no problem. After leaving the gun shop, we came to a restaurant that looked inviting so we went in for a much-needed source of protein.

After a thick ribeye steak, cooked rare with all the trimmings, we walked by a movie theater. We looked at all the movie posters and noticed all these movies had run back home about 2 years ago. Still, we enjoyed looking at them and remembering the movies we had seen." The Train Robbers" with John Wayne was the Now Playing movie. We hadn't seen it, so we decided we were in no hurry, might as well enjoy the movie.

We paid the $3 for the two of us at the window in the front booth, as we opened and went through the doors, we were hit with the aroma of popcorn and butter that is ever-present in movie theatres and nowhere else.

We found some seats in the small ten-rows theatre. Each row had only eight seats. A small balcony with a few seats overlooked the screen. There was a slight smell of mildew mixed with the popcorn in the dimly lit room. The movie started with a cartoon, and then on to the main event. John Wayne was fantastic as always, even though the director attempted to somehow make the old west hip.

We headed back to the motel, as we were ready for some much-needed sleep after those weeks of endless toil at the ranch. John began to run a fever and had some stomach discomfort that evening. Early the next morning we repacked the Jeep and got started. We headed for the mountains and some more breathtaking wilderness.

We followed the road from Prince George east toward the Rocky Mountains and the city of Jasper, we then expected to head north to continue our quest of the Yukon. At the entrance to Jasper National Park, we stopped and put lead seals on our rifles. John was still pretty tired so Jim did most of the driving. After a while, John wanted to stop, as he didn't feel well, so we pulled over and he got sick. John's condition was deteriorating very rapidly, after a couple of hours he was incoherent and began blacking out between vomiting episodes.

Jim began to be very concerned and felt we needed to get help. Jim told John we needed to find a hospital, John reacted violently and said just stop at a drug store so we could get something for his stomach.

Jim kept driving looking for a drug store and John kept getting worse. Jim decided to head toward the biggest town in the vicinity to ensure there would, not only be a drug store but also other help if needed. He swung the Jeep around and instead of heading north for the Yukon we were now heading south for Calgary.

It took several hours of hard mountain driving to reach Canada's HYW-1, to point's east. We passed through Calgary about one in the morning without finding a single thing opened, so Jim kept the Jeep headed east, only stopping to put gas in the tank from a jerry can.

John woke up a couple of times in the next several hours, giving Jim just enough warning to get to the side of the road. He was still delirious during these stops, once he saying he needed to get a motel room until this passed.

We arrived in Brooks just before dusk. Jim spotted a rather run-down little motel where the NO wasn't lit up alongside a lighted "VAC. It looked as modest as our funds so he pulled in. The clerk or owner was an extremely gaunt-looking fellow with a very large and raged cowboy hat on. He picked at his teeth with a large knife when Jim entered the office. "What can I do fer ya, young fella," he said with a scowl on his face. I replied, "have you got a room available?" A large smile came over his face and he said, "Sure do!" that will be nineteen dollars for the night, how long are you gonna stay?" Knowing our cash flow situation, Jim answered just one night. He handed Jim the keys to number six and he proceeded to unpack the absolute essentials from the Jeep. The last thing that he removed was John who was momentarily conscious, stumbling along beside Jim.

After a couple of hours of trying to watch the fuzzy broken TV in the hotel room and trying not to disturb John, Jim decided to take five dollars from our now meager kitty and take a look around town. He walked toward what looked like the town center, passing several Quonset hut-type structures that looked like they had been abandoned many years ago, except for the heavily worn paths to and from the doors and parking areas in front of them. He also passed a very large implement supplier whose yard had rows and rows of old farm equipment with grass growing up around the tires and rusting like a well-organized junkyard. Very close to the building sat two brand new harvesting machines that looked out of place in this dilapidated place. Rounding the corner past the implement dealer sat a large single-story brick building with a wooden sign bolted above the front door reading "Community Center Welcome" on it.

Jim heard laughter and the mild drone of a crowd in conversation. It was just what he needed at that moment, to be welcome so he went inside. He noticed a large well-lit room full of cafeteria-style bench tables, with groups of people in casual conversation. Malt and hops filled up our lungs and tempted Jim with beer. He sat down at an empty table and began looking around. The place was full of young people mostly slightly older them him. They were all socializing and having beers.

I was not old enough to drink in Canada, so I just sat and watched the people for a while. A group next to my table noticed me sitting there and asked if I would care to join them. I quickly accepted and moved to their table. They asked where I was from, and when I told them I was from Chicago, they lit up with enthusiasm and began to ask me about gangsters. I told them that the gangsters they heard about hadn't been around since the '20s and that I was really from a northern suburb. This didn't matter to them they were excited to talk to someone that was from anywhere other than this town. We talked for hours. Someone bought a pitcher of Labatt's beer on tap and an extra glass on the sly for me, and they asked me about all aspects of our trip.

The community center closed about midnight so Jim thanked them for their hospitality and headed back to the motel. He found John exactly where he left him. John took a look at the map and decided we should head east. We were low on money and still hadn't found a drugstore. Jim checked our fuel supply. Both jerry cans were full and had about a half a tank in the Jeep which would take us about 450 miles. From the looks of the map, we needed every bit of it.

The next morning, Jim grabbed the box of canned food and utensils out of the back of the Jeep and put them on the passenger seat making sure that all our cassette tapes were in easy reach. He loaded John in the back, and got back on the Queens highway A1, heading east.

We rode all day and into the night, looking for the next big town that might have a drug store for John. Again, and again, we came through small towns one after another. The next bigger town we went through was at 2:00 A.M., without anything open. Jim took another look at the map and determined we would be near Regina early in the morning. Surely, they would have a drug store.

As the sun began to rise, a sea of gold wheat lay before us as far as they could see in all directions with nothing else except the road in front and behind. Finally, the tall spires of the skyline of Regina appeared like the scene from the *Wizard of Oz*: waving golden wheat all around, with this little spot, not unlike the Emerald City, rising in the distance.

It took another hour or so before we came to the city and found the drug store in the downtown area that John so badly needed. After getting Tums and some other antacids we got in the Jeep and headed back for the highway. John again passed out in the back.

Our funds were very low, so Jim stopped at a gas station and topped everything off. He decided that the best thing to do in our present state was to head home. He started a nonstop drive east. One night and day, then two nights and days. After about 48 hours, he was having some trouble staying alert, so he turned up the CCR on the tape player, poured water on his head from the canteen, and opened another can of cold pork and beans. The pile of empty cans was getting pretty deep on the floor of the jeep, but he kept ongoing. You would think that after this much time things would start to well, let's say smell a little pungent in the cramp surroundings. But this was a jeep with a soft top and factory-made drain holes just above the floor on each side. There was no problem with ventilation. John came to every few hours, long enough to angrily say get a motel to which I would reply, "Next one that I see," and he would pass back out. We didn't have the money for another night in a motel and I wanted to get him back home as soon as I could. There was no need to call home because there would have been nothing that could have been done to change the situation.

In the middle of the third night, with Golden Earring's "Radar Love" cranked up, Jim suddenly became alert again, second wind or just way over-tired, but it was a welcome relief.

The next morning the terrain transitioned to large rock formations surrounded by clusters of trees dotting the landscape. As we continued, the forest thickened with larger, and larger pine trees. The rock formations became larger as well, causing the road to becoming more contoured. As we continued, east we passed countless ponds nestled in between the rocky mounds and outcroppings.

Emo, Ontario

We had to get some gas and check the map. A road sign revealed the town of Kenora 85 km ahead so Jim decided that would be the place to take a break. We came into town and he spotted a combination gas station sporting goods store so he pulled up to the pump. He filled the tank and one jerry can. He went inside to pay. As the clerk handed Jim the change, he realized that this was just about all the money we had left. He browsed around a bit and an old gentleman in the back asked him if he needed a new fishing rod. The guy explained that he makes custom-made, to a customer's specific preference and that he could whip one up for Jim in about an hour. Jim thanked him for his trouble but said he was just looking around.

When Jim got back to the Jeep John was awake and asking where we were. Jim told him it looked like we were about 20 minutes from the border. John climbed into the front seat and we headed for Minnesota.

We reached the border where a line of about five cars in front of us moved quickly After about 5 minutes, we pulled up to the guard. He took a look at us and looked inside the Jeep and said pull into that garage and pointed to the open overhead door in the row of five doors. As we slowly pulled in and stopped, someone said to turn off the engine, you are going to be here a while. The overhead door started to slowly close. In front of us was a closed overhead door with three customs agents standing in front of the door and one behind us operating the door. The customs agents began looking over the Jeep and one of them asked us to get out and said to stand in a spot that was marked on the floor. It appeared they were assessing what they were going to do and what tools they were going to use from the large assortment on the benches along each side of us: power tools that would rip, tear, cut, and open anything on a vehicle. They could get into any space, no matter how small. One agent questioned Jim, as the other three continued to inspect the Jeep. Eureka! One agent exclaimed after only a minute or two, what is this? He held up one of the dozens of roll-your-own cigarette butts that littered the floor of the Jeep. John said it's a cigarette, we had been rolling our own ever since we ran out of the U.S. smokes, as the Canadian ones made us nauseous. Besides that, "one" he so proudly found, the other agents said, "They are everywhere." The ashtray is full of them and they are on both sides. There must be a hundred of them. If these are tobacco where are the makings, the one agent said? It's in there somewhere "Prince Albert in a can," I said.

They continued to search for 20 minutes but they were unable to find what they thought they'd find. It was around this point one of the agents said they should send the butts out for testing. They were kind of mad that there was so much garbage on the floor, as Jim has been eating canned goods for 4 days and just throwing the empties on the floor.

It wasn't like we were throwing the butts on the floor. They started in the ashtray and as the tray filled up, they fell out on the floor, and most of the time was sucked out through the water scuppers on the floor. More than likely, the ashtray was never emptied.

You knew we were coming to the border; you could have cleaned up, another agent said. All we could do now was apologize and asked if we could help look for Prince Albert can. Finally, they just gave up and said is there anything in there that we should know about! John said, well we do have four rifles. The agents looked dumbfounded and pissed, wherein the hell are, they? They couldn't believe they searched the vehicle for nearly a half-hour and didn't find any rifles.

Two of the agents now have their guns drawn and the other two were trying to figure out what to do. Not too many people offer up something the agents could not find so; this was beginning to be embarrassing for them.

The agents told John to pull them out. He moved the piles of stuff and pulled open the secret drawer under the bench seat and showed the agents where they were. As one agent pulled them out one at a time the others just stood there with their mouths wide open. We could tell this was just not the norm for them. Lucky for us the lead seals that were put on in Alberta were still intact. They said "put these back together and get out of here."

We thanked them for their blessing and headed on into Minnesota.

Minnesota

John looked much better and for the first time in nearly a week he said, I am hungry. Jim decided we needed a good breakfast so he pulled into the first cheap-looking diner he saw. The parking lot was crowded The Jeep's wheels sunk into the fresh gravel as he turned sharply, finding a spot under some pine trees on the north end of the lot.

As we walked in, we were greeted by the pungent smell of fresh coffee. We saw the place was lively and full so we headed to the only two seats left at the counter. Everyone was in great spirits and we heard many conversations and laughter rising from most of the tables.

We ordered the special eggs and pancakes. The smell of the pancakes was incredible, sweet and rich, like a bakery, rather than a small backwoods diner. The meal hit the spot and it was sure good to have two people in conversation after all those days and miles of just one man at the wheel.

We paid the check and tipped leaving us about 90 cents between us, but for some reason, we didn't care. We were back in the U.S. and had enough gas to get to Manistique, where we would have a place to clean up and sleep.

Manistique, Michigan

Jim's family had a summer cabin on the beach in the upper peninsula of Michigan, near the town of Manistique. When he was about 11 years old his parents purchased the thickly wooded lot that ran from a small gravel road about 400 feet down to the water of Lake Michigan. That first year, they were able to camp on some property a half-mile down the beach and his father, brother, and a family friend spent a week cutting trees and brush to provide an opening onto the property, just to set up a path for a contractor to build the driveway to the beginning of the beach the area where they would build a cottage.

Jim's parents paid off the property and then began the build of the cottage his father had designed. Over his high school years, he spent many weekends building garages and doing other carpentry side jobs with his father. That was how his parents funded the cottage build.

Jim's father hired a contractor to dig the foundation, pour the footings and build the cement block basement so that when the family arrived on my father's 2-week vacation from work, we could build the first floor. Unfortunately, when we arrived, we found a tractor sitting in a hole without having done the complete excavation, not to mention the footings or basement. Jim's father went to town to call the lumber yard to cancel the wood delivery, that we needed for the first floor and began trying to contact the contractor. We drove over to his house on Indian Lake, and my father talked with him. Ole, the contractor insisted he would be out in the morning to move the project along.

When Ole Olsen arrived the next morning, he stood beside our campfire all morning and talked to Jim's father and he was getting frustrated. Ole finally went over and began slowly digging with the tractor to get the grade for the footings. The work went very slowly. At lunch he decided to take a break, Jim's father accepting the situation, offered him a beer. Ole, happily accepted the beer, and from that point on began working at a much faster pace. Ole, was shorthanded as his helpers were out for the week fishing, so my father volunteered my older brother Rick who was 15 years old, and myself who was two years younger to fill in as laborers for the day.

The flatbed carrying the concrete blocks arrived, and the driver relayed the story of how he was ticketed on his way for being overloaded. He tried to make the 60-mile journey from the brickyard in one load, but they needed just a little more than the weight limit on the truck. The truck was not able to pull in the driveway, so, the two boys started unloading the truck. After a few hours, the boys unloaded and had carried the blocks 200 feet to the building site. Jim got assigned to the portable mixer. He mixed mortar as fast as he could per Ole's instructions, and his brother carried mortar and bricks to Ole. The foundation and basement walls were completed quickly because Ole kept working as long as he had a beer.

Over the next few years, Jim's family spent their vacations building the wood frame cottage, lifting the large mortise and tendon beams into place supporting the structure and roofline. Jim installed the lucky pine tree at the peak when they reached that part of the construction. He was the only one in the family that would brave the heights.

The cottage would be our destination and refuge as it was as far as our fuel and dwindling funds would take us. We were in high spirits as we headed southeast and reached the outskirts of Duluth. We continued into Wisconsin, along the Lake Superior coast toward the U.P. (Upper Peninsula) of Michigan on US-2.

Once in Michigan we slowly cut across the U.P. East on US 28 to 41 through Marquette, then south another 90 miles back onto US2 to Manistique. As we neared Duck-in-Road the road that took us to the gravel road that was the remaining 8 miles to our destination, we got excited and relieved to have made it this far. We headed on the gravel down to the lake and turned to follow what had turned into a washboard from lack of grading and maintenance. There was a chain stretched across the driveway secured with just a hook for security.

Because Jim was driving, John got out and unhooked the chain and pulled it to the side. Instead of climbing back in the jeep, John decided to sit on the hood and ride in from there.

As we pulled into the overgrown driveway, we could see the dunes and the stairs leading up to the door. It was about there that we hit a hole or a log in the driveway that sent John flying into the air and slamming butt first hard on the hood of the jeep. He was feeling better but, there were a few parts of him with lingering effects of being sick for so long. He said a few things that he wasn't very proud of when he landed and to this day regrets saying. After all, Jim did just drive halfway across North America to get us here and I think he knew John was still not 100%!

After climbing out of the Jeep we were drawn to the sound of the surf and the smell of seaweed and wet sand that is Lake Michigan. We clamored over the dunes to the beach to take in the roar of the breaking waves and fresh lake breeze in our faces. We made it! We saw a lot of amazing people, places, and things since we left home, but this just took both of us back. We just stood there. Not saying a word for about five minutes.

John pulled our backpacks from the jeep, while Jim began turning over the rocks to find the hidden key his family always had just in case. He found the key and we went up the weathered stairs to the door. As we opened it, a rush of stale air hit us, as the cottage had been closed all winter. Immediately opening the front windows brought in a wave of moisture-laden cool air off Lake Michigan. After dropping his backpack in the bedroom, John went back down the stairs and headed for the woods and the reliable small wood structure with the hole in the center that campers and woodsmen know well. The outhouse.

After some relief and settling in, we went through the cabinets to see what provisions were available. Our hunger was now beginning to grow and our Jeep larder depleted from the last leg of our journey. We had a large jar of marinara sauce in our supplies, paired nicely with the pasta noodles we found in the cabinet. Spaghetti for dinner.

We wanted to celebrate our arrival, so we remounted the Jeep to head to town. With our last 90 cents we got a beautiful sweet onion and some carrots. Jim thought the carrots would work great in the sauce. A tip he learned in boy scouts from an old army cook and a scout leader. The carrots in the sauce would neutralize the acid in the tomatoes. We needed to add something else to provide more sustenance. Jim also hoped this trick might make the meal a little easier on John's stomach.

While we were out, we made collect calls to our family, asking for some funds to get us enough gas to cover the remaining 370 miles to get home. John had about one hundred and fifty dollars in savings and asked his dad to close the account and send us the money. He agreed to send the cash first class and said it would take two or three days to get there. This would be enough to get us home. Then we called our girlfriends to let them know where we were. They were so happy to hear from us. They wanted to come up and see us because we told them we did not know when we would be home due to being out of money. We were guessing maybe a week or so. Well, that didn't set very well with them and they politely agreed to the week or two. We had no idea they were planning on surprising us with a road trip. They might have been planning this for a long time because it didn't take them long to put the trip together.

We had a very filling meal that night. We saved what leftovers we had in the gas refrigerator in the kitchen because we knew we would be eating it for a while.

The next day we again made the trip back to town to go to the post office. Sure, enough the gun shop in Prince Edward B.C. had sent John's pistol to general delivery and it was waiting at the post office in a brown paper wrapped box with a string tied around it like a charismas package. We could hardly believe they were able to mail it across the border with the gun powder and primers.

Since we had some time to kill Jim said, I should take their new family toy out for a ride. The three-wheeler, ALSPORT Tri-Sport with an 18.5 HP Rockwell JLO engine did 65 mph with your feet on the front wheel pegs and your butt about 8 inches off the ground, it had soft dune tires that were perfect for the beach. They also helped get across some of the small creeks feeding into the lake.

With a full tank of gas, and a two-minute orientation, John was ready to go. In hindsight, he should have thought about safety. But off he went. Down the drive to the washboard gravel road. He could see for about a quarter mile each way and all was clear.

Let's see what this thing can do. It had no gears to shift, just a throttle and clutch. Slowly he letting out the clutch, good. Twisting the grip for the throttle fast, not so good. The front tire slowly lifted off the ground and proceeded to rise as John increased the gas. He wasn't sure if at that moment he wanted to back off or to see how high the tire would go but there was a moment that said slow down tiger when I saw a car coming at me head-on with a trail of dust coming off the back tires. What the hell.

We were in the middle of nowhere. Where did this guy come from? So, John backed off the gas and the front tire slammed down in the gravel and because there was no fender on the front wheel the gravel flew up and hit every part of his body except for his feet. The only "safety" gear he had was his sunglasses and a pair of cut-off blue jeans. No injury no foul. He saw the car fly by him without even slowing down. The driver must have been a logging truck driver and been used to "owning the road."

Well, enough with engaging the public. Back to the driveway... at sixty miles per hour. Yes, Jim was right, this thing could fly. Down the drive, past the stairs to the second floor, a quick wave to Jim sitting on the deck and into the dunes and onto the beach. Up and down the perfectly flat coarse sand beach John drove. Their property is on one of only a few natural coves with this type of sand. Most of the beaches were round-washed stone. Every so often, John skimmed over a shallow stream coming out of the woods going onto the Lake. His skills were now pretty good at this point.

The unpredictable dunes were John's next challenge. The other side was a wildcard until he is right at the top, the trike had the power to climb right up the dunes that were much like the Lake Michigan waves. Sharp and close together, not spread out over a large area. John went up one and down through the trough to the next crest. That's when he came upon a washed-out tree stump down in the trough. Unlike a stump a farmer might pull out of his field, his stump was washed out of the sand with all its roots still intact: sun-dried, bright white, hard driftwood. The only way he could see his way out of this was to give the trike all the gas he could and try and jump over the stump to the next crest. Whew! He made it! Except for the balloon tires on the back. Instead of digging in, they bounced him back onto the stump, upside down with the three-wheeler on top of him still running.

It took a second for John to figure what was going on here. The engine was running and gas was dripping on him and he 'can't reach the kill switch. He broke off a piece of the root and pushed the button to kill the engine. That did not stop the gas problem, but one thing at a time; at least the tires weren't spinning anymore. John was pinned in such a way that he could not lift the machine off him so he dug out the sand until he could crawl out. It seemed like thirty minutes went by before he freed himself. He pulled the trike off the stump and flipped it over. It started right up. There didn't seem to be any damage, except to John's pride.

John took his time going back to the cabin. The need for risk had somehow evaporated. Jim was inside so John pulled into the lower part of the house that was the garage and closed things up. When he got up to the main part of the cabin Jim asked how I liked it and then said what happened in a very calm tone? I told him I flipped it on a dune but everything looks ok. He said that happens to everyone. When I asked him how he knew something happened he said my tee-shirt was full of blood and there was a piece of wood sticking out of my neck and blood was dripping out of the wound.

Jim went into medic mode and gathered the necessary items to perform crude surgery. A pair of pliers, a semi-clean rag, half a bottle of mercurochrome, and a pocketknife. He told John it would be better if he sat down because he did not know how close the wood was to John's jugular and he might, pass out when he pulled it out. After all, Jim did pull a bullet out of one of his brother's friends, Steve, with the same pocketknife. But that's an adventure for another day.

So down John sat while Jim prepared for the surgery. Clean the wound, check. Clean the tools, check. The last thing Jim said as he came at John with the pliers was, this may bleed a little or a lot. The wood was stuck in over one inch and Jim said it put up a little fight. Jim gave John a choice of closing up the wound with a hot poker from the wood-burning stove or trying his hand with stitches. John declined both.

The next day we drove back to the post office. Sure enough, there it was. The letter from John's dad that we were waiting for with the cash we desperately needed along with a note saying that Jim's parents invited them up to the cabin and thought it would be great to all get together for a few days. They would all be up there in one week.

That night we went into town and got a bite to eat and headed over to the bar for some well-deserved libation! The Harbor Bar was just what anyone might expect in an old paper mill town down by the harbor, hence the name. It was here we met an old merchant marine sailor that told the bartender to give us each beer and ordered us a couple of shots. He must have had some pull in there because the bartender did not bat an eye or ask for ID. He had some great stories that kept going the whole night. For the life of us, we can't remember any of the stories except he had been on Great Lake ships for 38 years and never had seen the ocean. We don't remember paying for a single drink that night!

We spent the next day enjoying the beach. That year the Alewives were not too bad and it helped that the wind was mostly coming from land, so it only took 20 minutes of raking to get them into a hole and bury them to get rid of the light dead fish smell. Just a laid-back day with no plans except to nurse a mild hangover. There is something about a long walk on the beach that opens your mind. From this point on we were going to go back to what was, and this was going the be the start of our lives without school as we knew it. If there were jobs available here, we think we might have stayed for some time.

The next morning started slowly with a good breakfast of bacon and eggs. We started cleaning up a bit because there was going to be a house full of people soon and we wanted the place to look the way it did when we found it.

It must have been early afternoon when we were startled by the sound of a horn outside. Our girlfriends and Jim's sister, Cathy, were pulling into the driveway in her Camaro to surprise us. Jim said, "I told you they were up to something!"

We were so glad to see them. After their long drive from Illinois, we all headed to the beach. Jim's sister's boyfriend had brought a case of beer even though he was not old enough to buy it. We enjoyed the rest of the day with them playing in the waves.

We were not away for long when you think about it, about three months or so. But for us, we were in our little bubble. We did not listen to the news or hear about current events much. We did not know what new albums came out or if there was a new movie released. So, when we were in the water splashing around, everyone was making these sounds like a horror movie, dun-dun, dun-dun, dun-dun. Then, like a bad water ballet, they were all jumping out of the water and thrashing about like they were being attacked by sharks. When they looked at us not having a clue what they were doing, they told us about a new movie called "Jaws." It would be several weeks before we would fully understand.

That night we had a bonfire on the beach, sharing stories of the things that we had done, the places we visited, and the people we had met while we were on our adventure. It was a good thing that earlier in the day before anyone arrived, we set up a couple of tents in the dunes in the anticipation of this moment.

In the morning, while we were eating breakfast, we started to talk about the events that happened at home while we were gone. Sadly, the only thing that stands out was the loss of one of our friends, Brian Elrich. He lived in the subdivision just west of ours across Rt 83. We met in high school through one of our friends, Dan Johnson. Dan lived on the corner of Rt 83 and South Dennis. They shared a common interest. Dan with his '47 Ford coupe and Brian with his '57 Chevy stock car he was working on. They also both had motorcycles, and it was while riding one night that Brian and another friend picked up a couple of girls while bar hopping. They were on their way to another hop when they rounded a corner and Brian hit a stop sign and both he and the girl were killed.

Manistique is a very small town of four thousand people and the kids in town during the summer cruise from the Ford dealer on the east end of town to Clyde's Drive-in near the west end of town. Clyde's is an amazing old drive-in with a small counter inside, and carhops to wait on the cars dining outside. On a nice day, we could sit under an umbrella at one of their picnic tables out front. They still served Pepsi in those blue or red-colored plastic tumblers, Cliff runs the place. He makes an amazing and famous "Big C" burger that we considered one of the very best. One of the things that make it stand out is the fact that it is the largest single-patty hamburger we had ever seen; three-quarters of a pound of ground beef with cheese inside and on top and all on a special oversized bun! It is so big that it was commonly split between a couple on a date. A challenge too tempting to be ignored for a growing teenage boy. They had a second location 70 miles to the north in St. Ignace, but Cliff's Manistique store is the best.

The next day we all decided to go to Clyde's.

The big day arrived. We did not know what time everyone planned to arrive but, it was about eight hours to drive. Our parents were early risers so, we guessed sooner rather than later. John's parents were going to bring their pop-up camper so we had no idea how long they were planning to stay. This was uncharted territory for all of us. Don't get us wrong. Our parents were friends. The dads were our scout leaders and had gone on many camping trips with the boys. But we never went on vacation as families.

They arrived like a caravan. Pulling off the road and down the driveway. Their windows were down and arms were sticking out waving like we have been gone for years. It was good to see them!

After everything was set up and unpacked, they pulled out the pictures we sent and news articles they saved. They also had a map of the route we took, as we told them where we had been. It took quite a while to explain everything they showed us but, it sort of justified the decisions we made on the trip. We thought it might be better not to tell them everything, just stick to what they asked about.

Illinois (Home Again)

The first few days back we felt so different. We had experienced freedom on a level that is hard to explain. The common territory we felt comfortable, was in either one of our two friends, Cliff's or Dan's garage. It was at Dan's one night, well into our second case of beer that someone came walking up the driveway. It was not uncommon for people to just drop by because anyone driving by on 83 could see if someone was out and about. There were no outside lights on so, you could not see who the silhouette was until the lights from the garage illuminated their face. It was Brian Elridge! Our friend, who we were told was killed in the motorcycle accident while we were gone.

Were we looking at a ghost? Did we somehow go back in time? Get real, it was just Brian walking up the drive. After cracking open another beer Brian started telling us, what he was told happened to him.

For starters, he doesn't remember anything from that night. Maybe, for him, that's a good thing.

He was told the night started like most, riding his motorcycle with friends, bar hopping, and picking up girls. But that night they were racing from one place to the next when he took a corner too tight and hit a stop sign. He then rolled up his sleeve and showed us a massive scar the whole length of his left bicep. His scar also had the bolt hole pattern from the stop sign post running right next to the wound that opened up his entire arm. The girl that was on the back, unfortunately, leaned over to see the turn they were making and was decapitated instantly. Brian was in a coma for quite a few weeks and then spent time recovering from other broken bones sustained that night. It wasn't until the doctors thought he could handle it that they told him of the fate of his passenger. We guessed that explained why no one knew he survived and just assumed he died that night.

After a couple of weeks of decompressing and running out of money, it was time to go back to work. John cleaned up and got a haircut and drove over to the machine shop in Rosemont where he used to work at. When he was about a block away, he knew something was off. There was construction going on everywhere for the new Rosemont Stadium. The street where the shop was, was gone. There was a fence and behind that a big open area like for a parking lot. It turned out the that is exactly what it was. The street, the building, and his job gone. No one knew where they moved to or if they just closed up. It was about two years later when John found out they did move, to Buffalo Grove. Three miles from Wheeling.

Over the next few years, John would have reoccurring sicknesses like the one when Jim was driving back to the US. There would be a high fever of 104 and he'd be delirious for two or three days. It would hit him like a ton of bricks every twelve months or so. There was a reoccurrence when he was working in a restaurant as a cook when the next attack hit. The entire third shift was at one of the waitresses' houses for a no-occasion party, as we called them when he could feel "it" coming on. There was no mistaking what was about to happen. John told his friend that he was not feeling well and asked if there was someplace, he could lay down for a little while. He explained that since our trip he would sometimes be out of it for a few days. Since the party was just getting started, she knew he was not drunk and said she had a couch in the basement that would be nice and private.

John woke up about forty-eight hours later with two or three people staring at him. One of them was his friends' husband. who used to be a medic in the army He told John, you were in sad shape and they were just getting ready to take him to the hospital when he started to come out of his comatose state. He said it sounded like it could be a parasite that was picked up in Canada and it would reoccur every so often. So, every time John came to and asked for a glass of water, he gave him tonic water. He said John must have drunk a quart in the past two days. No one knows if that was what the problem was but he did switch his drink of choice to a vodka tonic and that was the last time he was sick. We discovered that tonic water has "Quinine" in it, the same thing they used to treat Malaria.

We both needed to get a job. Jim was lucky enough to snag his old job back at the Auto parts store, working the counter and running the machine shop as he had been taught by the machinist when he worked there before our trip. After a few months of this, he began to get the urge for another adventure. He got together with John, and our friend Cliff.

Jim suggested that we go see a recruiter and join the Air Force. At this point, we had draft cards and thought it would be better to join the branch we wanted rather than get drafted, even though the draft had pretty much ended at that point. Cliff immediately objected to the Air Force as he wanted to go in a branch that had Jeeps. I convinced him that the Air Force had Jeeps and that I was sure he would get to drive them. We all went to the recruiter the next day and enlisted with guaranteed jobs as mechanics, although the fine print explained had a very broad definition. We found that out later.

Jim told his employers of his plan and they decided they did not need him if he was going to leave again after such a short time back. So, the 6 weeks until we had to report, Jim was unemployed. He spent most of his time working on an engine swap in his pickup truck. He sold the jeep to John's father and felt good to know it was going to a good home. Years later when he returned from Southeast Asia, his parents surprised him with it. They bought it back from John's dad. The plexiglass windshield was replaced with custom-made auto glass. What a much-appreciated bonus.

Play List

Bachman-Turner Overdrive (BTO) - *Not Fragile* **(1974)**
 1 "Not Fragile"
 2 "Rock Is My Life, and This Is My Song"
 3 "Roll On Down the Highway"
 4 "You Ain't Seen Nothing Yet"
 5 "Free Wheeling"
 6 "Sledgehammer"
 7 "Blue Moanin'"
 8 "Second Hand"
 9 "Givin' It All Away"

Creedence Clearwater Revival (CCR) - *More Creedence Gold* **(1973) Cassette Tape**
 1 "Hey Tonight"
 2 "Run Through The Jungle"
 3 "Fortunate Son"
 4 "Bootleg"
 5 "Lookin' Out My Back Door"
 6 "Molina"
 7 "Who'll Stop The Rain"
 1 "Sweet Hitch-Hiker"
 2 "Good Golly Miss Molly"
 3 "I Put A Spell On You"

4 "Don't Look Now (It Ain't You Or Me)
5 "Lodi"
6 "Porterville"
7 "Up Around The Bend"

Grand Funk Railroad – *Closer to Home* (1970)
1 "Sin's a Good man's Brother"
2 "Aimless lady"
3 "Nothing Is The Same"
4 "Mean Mistreater"
5 "Get It Together"
6 "I Don't Have To Sing the Blues"
7 "Hooked on Love"
8 "I'm Your Captain/Closer to Home"

Golden Earing - *Moontan* (1973)
1 "Candy's Going Bad"
2 "Are You Receiving Me"
3 "Suzy Lunacy"
4 "Radar Love"
5 "Just Like Vince Taylor"
6 "Vanilla Queen"

Eagles – Eagles (1972)
1 "Take it Easy"
2 "Witchy Women"
3 "Chug All Night"
4 "Most of Us Are Sad"
5 "Nightingale"
6 "Train Leaves Here This Morning"
7 "Take the Devil"
8 "Early Bird"
9 "Peaceful Easy Feeling"

10 "Tryin'"

Queen – *Sheer Heart Attack* November (1974)
1 "Brighton Rock"
2 "Killer Queen"
3 "Tenement Funster"
4 "Flick Of The Wrist"
5 "Lily Of The Valley"
6 "Now I'm Here"
7 "In The Lap Of The Gods"
8 "Store Cold Crazy"
9 "Dear Friends"
10 "Misfire"
11 "Bring Back That Leroy Brown"
12 "She Makes Me (Stormtrooper in Stilettoes)"

Deep Purple - *Machine Head* March (1972)
1 "Highway Star"
2 "Maybe I'm a Leo"
3 "Pictures of Home"
4 "Never Before"
5 "Smoke On The Water"
6 "Lazy"
7 "Space Truckin"

ACKNOWLEDGEMENTS

Acknowledgements

We would like to primarily thank our wives, who are both named Debbie for their ongoing support over the past twenty-five years. Without their encouraging comments like, "Are you done yet?" we would never have continued to keep writing down our thoughts. Just kidding, they didn't say that, wink, wink. They were supportive during our zero-days that could last for years, to our endless hours of writing when we were in the mood. We never would have continued unless we saw the excitement in their eyes each time another thought was put into print.

I was great fun reliving the trip of a lifetime, and finely getting all our thought into print. That is great if you are writing a logbook, but we wanted something that would allow the reader to come along on the journey. With the forgiving guidance and patience of a saint, Adela Crandell Durkee, an author of many books and publications came into the picture. We are not sure if she knew what she was getting into, but without her guidance and goal-setting, we never would have gotten over the hump to stick with and finely get it done.

- Jim and John

BIOGRAPHIES

Biographies

John Bruhn's love of the outdoors began with childhood family camping trips to Door County Wisconsin. As he grew older those family trips grew into ski trips to the slopes of Colorado. In his twenty's a new adventure began, starting a family. This brought him a son, John Jr, and a daughter Amy. The love of the outdoors was passed on to them. In 1991 John met his second wife, Deborah and her daughter Christy. Their adventures together morphed into glamping, boating, and international travel. They joined the US Coast Guard Auxiliary. As one of their classmates said "If you join the

Auxiliary all the classes are free." Today he does regular safety patrols on Lake Michigan and teaches boating safety.

Jim Julison's spent summer vacations in the Upper Peninsula of Michigan where he and his siblings helped their father build a cabin on the lake. As a child, Jim loved spending time alone exploring miles of deserted Lake Michigan coast line, and pine forest. Jim may have inherited some of his lust for adventure from his mother, a global traveler and writer. Jim began his biggest adventure when he married Deborah and started a family. He and his family worked hard building their dream home just outside of Marengo Illinois, where he and his wife still live with their attack golden doodle Daisy. Jim still enjoys working on old Jeeps and dreaming of new adventures for him and Deborah.

Today as both John and Jim turn 65 they are planning the next big adventure of section hiking the Ice Age Trail in Wisconsin.